B&T
$3.95

D0871705

LIVING FAITHS AND ULTIMATE GOALS

LIVING FAITHS
and
ULTIMATE GOALS

Salvation and World Religions

Edited by S. J. Samartha

Wingate College Library

Copyright © World Council of Churches, 1974

First U.S. Edition, ORBIS BOOKS, Maryknoll, New York 10545

Library of Congress Catalog Card Number: 75-7610

ISBN: 0-88344-297-3

Manufactured in the United States of America

CONTENTS

067305

8673b3

INTRODUCING A DISCUSSION

S. J. SAMARTHA [1]

The nine papers brought together here, with this introduction, are the fruit of cooperation between a number of friends who, while committed to differing religious and ideological persuasions, have joined in the common exploration of a theme we all feel to be vital and urgent: what is the ultimate goal of human life?

Christians here speak of 'salvation'. The initial reason for compiling this collection of essays was the world conference on mission and evangelism held at Bangkok from 29 December 1972 to 8 January 1973 [2] on the theme 'Salvation Today', and the inclusion of some of this material among the working documents of the conference was meant to help the delegates work on this profound issue in awareness of the diversity of cultural backgrounds and the plurality of commitments that characterize the world of today.

Another, more lasting reason has to do with the growing dialogue between people of living faiths and ideologies. This is of course taking place in all sorts of different settings around the world. For its part, the World Council of Churches has initiated dialogues at the world level [3] and has been following with close interest a number of national and regional initiatives, not least those of the Christian study centres. Many different themes have come up in discussion, and it now seems appropriate to try to concentrate debate on a particular issue. What could be more central, and common — whatever our different formulations of it — than the experience and understanding of salvation, especially at a time when technological civilization leads to sharp questioning of the meaning of personal life and the significance of human community? That already indicates why the thrust of 'ideologies',

---

[1] Dr STANLEY J. SAMARTHA, Church of South India, is the Director of the World Council of Churches' programme on Dialogue with People of Living Faiths and Ideologies.

[2] See *The Ecumenical Review*, Vol. XXV, No. 2, April 1973, 'Ecumenical Diary', and *International Review of Mission*, Vol. LXII, No. 246, April 1973.

[3] See *Dialogue Between Men of Living Faiths*, papers presented at a consultation held at Ajaltoun, Lebanon (Geneva : WCC, 1971), and *Living Faiths and the Ecumenical Movement* (Geneva : WCC, 1971), both ed. S. J. Samartha.

particularly of Marxism in its several varieties, is essential to the discussion. All classical conceptions of religious salvation are today being seriously challenged by revolutionary change. No human issue can be regarded as in some way 'exclusively religious'. All of us, whatever our situation, and whatever our persuasion, need to enlarge our horizons if we would share in the debate at the world level as active participants and not merely look on as disinterested spectators.

The inclusion of essays from the point of view of traditional religions of Africa, of Latin American Marxism and of China helps to widen and deepen the debate yet further.

I must also be sure to point out the inevitably limited scope of the collection. None of the authors is to be regarded as an official spokesman or 'representative' of the particular community or tradition from within which he thinks and writes. While the general theme and purpose of the collection was suggested to them, each author chose his particular title, as well as the approach that he follows. The common debate is made more difficult of course by the complexities of the very terms 'faith', 'religion' and 'ideology', whether in the singular or in the plural, let alone as translated into different languages and cultural settings. This is not the place to try to clarify these complexities ; enough perhaps to say that the phrase 'living faiths and ideologies' is intended to show that our concern is not so much with the objective, classical data of dogma and ritual in the great religious traditions as with those enduring and renascent elements which actually sustain and direct the lives of people today. The emphasis is more on the faiths men and women live by than on the religions or communities to which they belong. Up to each of us to say to what extent traditional views are proving unacceptable to new generations, which selected values and in which transformations are proving to be of decisive influence on contemporary attitudes, and how far the traditional boundaries are being blurred as people live together and indeed cross over those boundaries. We asked the authors to write out of the personal commitment they in fact live by, out of their own personal involvement in the life of their society and country, and out of their concern for the deeper, common issues of human existence as a whole. Our main purpose and justification for preparing what can only be a tentative collection is that it may help many to think out and deepen their faith in the context of a readiness for dialogue that cannot but become more and more crucial for all mankind in the years ahead.

Past and present

Some of the essays here seek to reinterpret lasting values in the classical religious traditions. Thus Dr Sivaraman discusses the meaning of *moksha* and Professor Abe that of *nirvana* for men of today, whether in the East or in the West. So too the essay on the Jewish conception of redemption takes into account the contemporary realities of the Middle East. But they also make unmistakably clear the living link between the past and the present. It would surely be irresponsible to seek the meaning of salvation *today* without at the same time trying to understand what it has meant to millions of people in the long stream of their cultural history *yesterday*. One cannot catch a glimpse of the dawn of tomorrow without looking for it within a certain structure of time and history, against the background of yesterday and today. Where, then, amid the fallen debris and broken idols, are the enduring values in classical traditions which can help us towards liberation from the bonds of the present ?

Some more recent strivings radically reject the past in their demands for change and hopes for the future. Mr Roy's essay on Marxism brings out the challenge which contemporary ideologies lay down, both as theories of deliverance and as techniques of liberation — and not in some distant future but here, today, now. Ideologies such as Marxism and Maoism have in our time imbued many with a burning sense of righteous indignation and with the courage to fight against tyranny and injustice by providing visions of the future of man and society which can direct and sustain the lives of millions. It would therefore be both unwise and unrealistic to exclude ideologies from any serious discussion on salvation today.

Moreover it would be foolish to overlook the contemporary interaction between 'living faiths' and 'ideologies', whether in those deeper layers of thought where fundamental issues are embedded or in the sphere of urgent action which does not permit over-scrupulous regard for theoretical lines of demarcation. At a time when life is dominated by science and technology, experiences of alienation and an awareness of transcendent dimensions can bring the two more closely together than either can normally imagine in the monologues of their separate camps. The very meaning or meaninglessness of life, for example, cannot be discussed without taking into account the fact of death. Even the most crying needs only take on significance within a horizon of meaning. Whether death is understood as *finis* or as *telos*, as the end of a line or the temporary closing of a recurring cycle, has a good deal to do with the presence or absence of a sense of urgency in seeking after salvation today. The fact that such topics as transcendence and death are being seriously discussed within certain ideologies is an indication that there are basic issues on which dialogue between people of 'living faiths' and those who follow 'ideologies' is not only possible but actively welcomed.

Moreover, one of the consequences of the recovery among Christians of a self-critical conscience about the colonial era is the awareness that religious attitudes, whether in theological formulations or in missionary actions, can all be riddled with conscious or unconscious ideological elements. In sociological terms ideology can be defined as a set of teachings or symbols generated by a society in order to protect itself against others, legitimate its power and defend its privileges. It thus produces divisions into 'we' and 'they'. The 'we' group — not necessarily Western or Christian — is constantly tempted to set itself over against the 'they' groups and to regard them as inferior. In this connection it is high time that the term 'non-Christian' be banished from our vocabulary. To use a merely negative term for vast numbers of our neighbours, many at least as intelligent and spiritually sensitive as any Christian, is nothing less than offensive. The expression is an ideological residue of theological colonialism. It leaves a bad taste in the mouth. Further, it lumps together in one bundle such radically different traditions as those of Islam and Buddism or Judaism and Hinduism, which may well differ more from each other than they do from Christianity. Worst of all, as Fr Panikkar never tires of reminding us, to talk of 'non-Christians' usually implies an estimate of these other religions as 'false'. If all religions are 'true', dialogue is hardly necessary. If only one religion is 'true', dialogue is impossible. No, the question is rather how, in a world of many living faiths and ideologies, men and women can best work together on the basic issues of human life. We need not often talk about dialogue itself, but the climate which genuine dialogue produces provides the indispensable climate of trust and freedom in which the real issues can be appropriately raised and discussed.

A variety of approaches

A common difficulty for such a discussion lies in the variety of approaches to what is meant by salvation, to the means of realizing it and to its consequences in the lives of men. This is of course far more than a matter of terminology : it goes deep into the varying analyses of the human situation and the differing visions of human destiny. Sivaraman, explaining *moksha* from the point of view of a Hindu theist, describes it as 'liberation from pain, suffering and loss, from estrangement of every kind. From the dubious and vulnerable character of human existence ... It is the freedom of enjoying union with God ... It is genuine self-affirmation rather than self-negation that is entailed by God-affirmation. Saving knowledge is of the nature of overcoming alienation.' There are, of course, different ways to attain this and the Hindu points to the well-known ways of knowledge, devotion and works. Askari, a Muslim, looks at it from a different point of view. Salvation is salvation from alienation. 'Alienation is breathlessness, panting, and gasping for time. Now freedom is just the ability to run fast ... To utter the word "God" is to raze to the ground the edifice of pseudo-eternity, to declare again that man is free.' He goes on to say, 'God's love in the Qur'an seems to be incomparably vaster than what the Old Testament contains regarding the love of God. Man is alienated from God, but God is not alienated from man.' Jenkins, speaking as a Christian, emphasizes that 'salvation is ultimately the giving of God himself to men so that their humanity is infinitely filled and fulfilled'. His opening sentence already contains the seed of his whole article : 'To be human is the gift of God.' But without a certain particularity, general statements about 'the ulti-mate richness of what it is to be human' cannot be really meaningful. Therefore he affirms, 'Jesus Christ is the decisive evidence offered to the faith of Christians and for the faith of Christians. He confirms to us that the activity of God Himself ensures that particular moments, historical processes and embodied persons are the places where God is met, known, received and responded to. This activity of God is His universal and all-embracing work of bringing about salvation, i.e. union with Him and with all fulfilled things and persons in Him.'

In the experience of dialogue this emphasis on *particularity* on the one hand and *humanization* on the other is likely both to enrich the experi-ence of the partners and to lead to a certain amount of confusion. For the word 'humanization', dangerously familiar perhaps to many Chris-tians in ecumenical discussion, is not so familiar in other settings and can be taken in several ways. It can be misunderstood by many Hindus to whom it is not the human but the divine in man that is significant. In certain streams of Hindu thought salvation is seen as a process by which the potentially divine in a man becomes actual and thus enables him to 'realize' his true nature. In the experience of salvation man is 'spiritualized'; he becomes divine. Again, it can be understood in a 'theological' sense as in the Eastern Orthodox tradition where, through 'theosis', man participates by grace in the divine-human nature of Christ and thus is restored to the full manhood God intends. In a 'secular' sense the term is limited to movements of economic, social and political liberation or to the processes of change brought about by science and technology. Strong opposition between this last and the earlier two are likely to make the debate difficult. Both in motivation and in purpose there is a big gap between them. On the other hand, the very search for new understandings of man and the struggle to bring about changes that may make the birth of a 'new humanity' possible are likely to lead to a new sense of the value of thinking, living and working together rather than in isolation.

A further point of frequent misunderstanding concerns the instrumental function of the community in the process of salvation. Ajit Roy maintains that 'the Marxist view of liberation is not concerned with one's individual quest for salvation in isolation from one's milieu. It is a perspective of man's fulfilment in the general stream of socio-historical evolution.' Again, Zwi Yaron, in explaining the contemporary Jewish understanding of redemption, says that 'God's promise of redemption includes the idea of the covenant between God and Israel ... and the theological implication of redemption: "And I will take you to Me for a people and I will be to you a God, and you shall know that I am the Lord your God" (Exodus 6 : 7).' He also points out that Jewish nationality has always had a theological significance for the Jews. 'Not only in the distant past was Jewish history unique, but this century, too, is pregnant with messianic indications.' Yet the notion of claiming any kind of uniqueness or exclusiveness is absent in the Hindu and Buddhist understandings of salvation. In Buddhism, for example, the emphasis is not on 'election' by which few are called and many left out but rather on the common sharing of human existence. Not only man, community and history but also nature, the whole cosmos and eternity are taken into account. Masao Abe points out that 'Christian personalism is connected with anthropocentrism. Contrary to this, Buddhist *nirvana* is based on egolessness and is not anthropocentric but rather cosmological. In Buddhism, man and nature are equally subject to change, transitory and transmigratory. Man cannot achieve emancipation from the cycle of birth and death until he can eliminate a more universal problem — the transcience common to all things in the universe.' Furthermore,

'Buddhist salvation is primarily concerned with individual persons, not necessarily man in general, for as it is written in a Scripture, "one is born alone, dies alone, comes alone, goes alone" (*The Larger Sukhavati Vyuha*).' This does not of course mean that the social consequences of *nirvana* are ignored nor that the community is neglected in the total dimension of Buddhist life. It is well known that the Buddhist *sangha* is one of the oldest community organizations by which religious values are conserved, discipline maintained and the Buddhist message spread abroad.

Individual and corporate

Thus the starting points and the emphases of these essays are by no means the same. The Hindu and Buddhist contributors draw attention above all to the bonds from which the individual must be delivered before experiencing the fullness of *moksha* or *nirvana*. Yet both are careful to point also to the social dimensions of this goal. The Jewish, Christian and Muslim contributors, on the other hand, all in their different ways bring out that salvation not only has social consequences but is indeed an intrinsically corporate affair. On this point the Marxist clearly belongs to this second group.

But we cannot neatly divide our partners into two categories, those who see salvation as individual and those who see it as social. The debate between the two emphases is often to be found within a particular community. Among Christians, for instance, this debate has often become controversial and divisive in recent years, involving acute differences on such questions as the authority of the Bible, the function of the Church, the practice of mission and the presuppositions of dialogue. Among those of other persuasions the debate has taken different forms and has varied in intensity, but the issues raised are not dissimilar. Seen in a worldwide horizon, there cannot but be some relationship between deliverance from the bonds of sin, ignorance and death, liberation from the chains of slavery, exploitation and injustice and the many ways by which men in all sorts of different cultures and situations have struggled to cope with their immediate needs in view of ultimate visions of a more abundant life. Now that we are all aware that we share a common future, dare we confine this debate to our own particular circle ? Jenkins' statement that saving is the work of God would be accepted by many of our partners. When he therefore says that the Church 'is neither the saving community nor the community of the saved, but rather the community of those who for the time being know (who at present embody the knowledge of) God the Saving one who is the Father of Jesus Christ', others without exactly agreeing may recognize what he is after. But in the light of what Sivaraman and Abe have said about the priority of the individual, can he be justified in concluding 'that there would be no meaning to and no meaning for salvation available in the world unless there were a community'?

In a pluralistic world, whether we like it or not, we are confronted by a situation of open variety, where any one persuasion is implicitly questioned by others. To avoid slipping into shallow relativism, each of us, Christians very much included, must face carefully the question of the central criterion of faith. Can we do this, individually and in the corporate striving of our community, without making genuine efforts to listen to what our neighbours of other living faiths and ideologies have to say about their understanding, their vision, their hope of salvation? This is precisely what we hope this collection can enable, if in a limited way: that we can all listen, however unfamiliar their categories, to the experience and commitments of others.

Two further questions

Any attempt to bring together different views on the true ends of mankind raises at least two further questions, which go beyond the sphere of methods and approach. Can that which is known as mysterious, holy and transcendent be described and communicated to people of other persuasions in rational and intellectual terms? Is not the experience of salvation something so deep, authentic and personal as to be essentially incommunicable and therefore unsuited to discussion or dialogue? The question is raised as between religious traditions and communities, but even more sharply when one of the partners is an ideology like Marxism to which the whole business of anything transcendent makes no sense. Dialogue with him on salvation may seem to be condemned before it ever starts. The second question is this: should the Christian who knows himself to be already saved spend time and energy in listening to other views, serious consideration of which is likely to endanger the purity of his faith or shake the steadfastness of his commitment? The attitude here presupposed, sometimes referred to as 'deaf self-sufficiency', is of course by no means confined to Christians. Others often display it too, in both open and more subtle forms. Jews, Muslims and Christians have all often been unwilling to listen to each other, let alone anyone else, because of the nature of the claims about each other which are involved in their origins. The Marxist, too, sure of the straightness of his ideological path, has often refused to listen to others lest his revolutionary energies be deflected. Despite their generous response to our invitation to write, our contributors may seem to be strange bedfellows.

Both questions raise such thickets of related problems — historical, theological and psychological — that I cannot here offer more than a few remarks. It is certainly true that the depth and fullness of any religion cannot be adequately conveyed by rational description, however fascinating in the intellectual sphere such descriptions may be. Wilfred Cantwell Smith, Professor of World Religions at Harvard University, sees fit to take serious notice of the arguments that 'any scholarly study of religion is inherently inadequate' and, conversely, that 'any study of religion is inherently unscholarly'.[4] To listen to others in this realm cannot only be a matter of listening to words but must involve being open and sensitive to the signs and symbols of religion used in contemplation or community worship. In some of the dialogues organized by the World Council of Churches we have sought to set the intellectual discussion of religious ideas into the larger context of the dimension of worship. On the other hand, without a serious intellectual engagement at the appropriate points between the partners of different living faiths and ideologies, the nature of the dialogue and the import of the issues confronting them can only remain blurred. It is vital to recognize that talking about salvation is for none of us equivalent to being saved, any more than comparing notes about prayer is the same as the act of praying. Yet the very urgency of the quest for new styles of meeting, new ways of reflecting theologically and new patterns of decision-making may lead us too easily to overlook the permanent need for strong, enduring and communicable ideas. People are held together by other and deeper means than by holding hands. Without the binding power of ideas that can be thoroughly discussed in personal debate, we who take up dialogue are only likely to become angels without wings, singing songs without words to harps without strings, lost in the happy clouds of misty celebrations.

Similarly, to the second question, there is a deeper reason for the need to listen to others than the unavoidable neighbourliness brought on by

---

[4] In *The Meaning and End of Religion.* New York : Mentor Books edition, 1964, p. 12.

modern technological developments. Many, in all our communities, are fearful of the consequences of modern civilization on our personal and corporate living. The relentless march of technology seems to threaten the very core of personal being and the living structure of shared life in human communities. Different cultures have traditionally related differently to nature and the environment. Responses to the machine different to those of the Hebrew-Christian tradition in which it largely originated seem to be possible. Can we help each other find ways of living out the meaning and mystery of life even while accepting all the benefits of modernity ? This is the real point of taking our neighbours in our multi-cultural, multi-religious and multi-ideological world seriously. The struggle between God and the idols, between Truth and its many distortions, is not to be pursued in a struggle between Christianity and 'other religions' ; it is one that is going on within every living faith, within every ideological community. This is why when people of different commitments come together in dialogue there is often a spontaneous discovery of comradeship and of a sense of converging purpose.

Two of the dialogues organized recently by the World Council of Churches, whose themes were in each case jointly formulated, took this up directly. The Consultation of Christians and Jews in late 1972 discussed 'The Quest for World Community — Jewish and Christian Perspectives',[5] while the Muslim-Christian dialogue earlier in the year had for its theme 'In Search of Human Understanding and Cooperation — Christian and Muslim Contributions'.[6] A third one held in April 1974 in Colombo, Sri Lanka, brought together about fifty people, Hindus, Buddhists, Jews, Christians and Muslims, to consider the theme 'Towards World Community : Resources and Responsibilities for Living Together'. Issues about new forms of community raised by science and technology on the one hand and ideologies like Marxism and Nationalism also entered into the debate.[7] In all these, far-reaching questions about the role of nations and religions in the search for world community came up time and time again and defied any easy answers. The global integration of humanity as a whole is no doubt a proximate, not an ultimate, goal, but to reach even that in justice, peace and fullness

---

[5] See *The Ecumenical Review*, Vol. XXV, No. 2, April 1973, 'Ecumenical Chronicle'.

[6] See *Study Encounter*, Vol. VIII, No. 3, 1972, SE/31.

[7] For the *Memorandum* of the Colombo Meeting see *Study Encounter*, Vol. X, No. 3, 1974, World Council of Churches, Geneva and for selected papers presented at the meeting see *The Ecumenical Review*, Vol. XXVI, No. 4, October 1974.

of life rather than by manipulation and new captivities, we shall have to pay careful heed to the deeper drumbeats of faith that echo in different parts of the world. That they may sound muffled, confused and contrasting is no excuse, at least for the Christian, not to open oneself to them.

This collection, then, is an invitation to listen in openness to some of our partners, hoping that they will be no less open to us. This openness is directed not just to their ideas about salvation, though these are what they are here writing about. It is concerned with them as people, with the many other people who think and believe more or less as they do, and in the last resort with God. To be open to God cannot mean prejudging the mind of God and erecting our own neat lines of demarcation as if we knew just where the Spirit of God is and is not at work. He is not bound by our prejudging. Nor is it to abandon commitment to the Truth as this has become known to us. It is, rather, gratefully to acknowledge that the fullness of Truth is always wider and deeper than our present apprehensions of it and that the Spirit is at work, in ways such that we do not know where He comes from nor where He is going, to guide us into all the Truth.

LIVING FAITHS
AND
ULTIMATE GOALS

THE MEANING OF *MOKSHA* IN CONTEMPORARY HINDU THOUGHT AND LIFE

K. SIVARAMAN [1]

I have been asked to discuss *moksha*, the Hindu counterpart of salvation, and its meaning for the 'contemporary' Hindu. In view of my specialized interest and supposed competence, my approach will be from the perspective of 'theistic' Hinduism. Accordingly, I wish first to comment briefly on 'contemporaneity' and, at more length, on 'theism' in relation to Hinduism. My comments will of course bear on the theme of *moksha*. I shall then analyse the implication of *moksha* by a bold appropriation of terms and ideas to which I have been exposed.

I

Does *moksha* have any meaning for the thought and life of the present-day Hindu ? The normal attitude is to treat it as part of traditional Hindu culture and therefore as accepted today, if at all, out of sheer cultural habit. It is true that many Hindus in their scholarly discussions exhibit this attitude. As in the rest of the world many Hindus too have no kind of contact with any form of religion or its modes of thought. They grow up as strangers to the terms and meaning of religion. If Hinduism as a living religion interests them little, its transcendent claims focused in a concept like *moksha* interest them even less.

But we do not have to search for a greatest or lowest common measure of acceptance in order to justify the claim of meaningfulness. To those to whom it is meaningful it is profoundly meaningful. To them, *moksha* is a living reality of their experience. The contemporary Hindu may not be exercised to the extent of prophesying about religious problems being the principal problem of the end of the century. But he certainly values *moksha*, whether actively or implicitly, and seeks to find a place for it in his view of human life and purposes. To many it presents itself as an 'esoteric' possibility open through submission to the rigour of spiritual discipline and discipleship. To some it is a kind of transient mystical ecstasy that is induced as the culmination of devotion, group-singing, meditation, etc. To the philosophically lettered, *moksha* is an abstract, formal, intellectual possibility and despite its abstractness, that is as

---

[1] Dr SIVARAMAN is Reader in Philosophy, Banaras Hindu University, India.

something that one has not yet 'had', its real value is still assumed as a possible experience for oneself.

All this is interesting as information but I do not think that these are the points which really concern us. What matters for contemporary Hindu thought is the Hindu self-understanding of his tradition in terms of growth and regeneration in response to the requirements of modern living and thinking. The contemporary Hindu is heir to systems of ideas of the Hindu East and of the non-Hindu West, both of which serve as sources of his way of looking at things. He achieves assimilation of the foreign not by a rejection of his own standpoint or ideal but by a deepening of it with increasing reverence through infinite patience and humility until what was foreign reveals its kinship with his own. The outcome is a reassessment of his heritage and a continual recreation or renewal of his faith. What remains 'traditional' about the tradition is its continuity, not its conservatism. Hindu tradition is a continuous process of evolution by a free use of reason and experience. This is how a Hindu, today, 'liberated' from his native medievalism, looks at his own faith. It is in this spirit that my personal reflections and reassessments of the meaning of *moksha*, quickened by closeness to a particular phase of Hinduism, are offered in this paper and made to pass for 'contemporary' views.

I now pass on to 'theistic' Hinduism. The theistic-absolutistic polarization of standpoints is one of the significant features of Hindu thought and life, and to accord recognition to this is to take a major step towards truly encountering Hinduism. Present from the very dawn of its history, this polarization emerged with greater self-consciousness and philosophic sophistication under the stimulus of the challenge of Buddhism.

The great divide between Hinduism and Buddhism seems to be, to put it in relation to our present concern, between the point of view according to which the love of a personal God is the very crown of the experience of liberation from bondage to which man has been subject, and a point of view where the love of God is acclaimed only as a preparation, even if a necessary one, for realizing the goal of such liberation. In both, it may be noted, liberation or deliverance stands for the ultimate goal of life's endeavour. The difference is in respect of what is entailed by the two standpoints, theoretically and also in practice. For the theist, spiritual liberation is identified with the love which becomes central and persuasive in the sphere of experience. God, none other than love itself (cf. the oft-quoted Tamil verse 'Love is God'), is the exact expression of perfect deliverance. God's self-revelation and man's liberation from self-estrangement coincide in the moment of the experience of love. The love of God means avowedly a corresponding love toward the concrete, individual, unique here and now. It is in the meeting of these two that *moksha* liberates and enlarges human existence. In contrast, the absolutist sees 'liberation' as, unequivocally, liberation from time, from the world and all that is conditioned by time. Spiritual liberation, itself no doubt a positive experience as the perfect expression of self or self-hood, is negative in respect of all those values associated with human life : history, personality, freedom, community, progress, etc. Self is, precisely, 'not this, not this'.

II

What gives a real edge to the 'absolutist' Hindu attitude is his severely theoretical veto of everything that is 'not-self'. Falsity — this is his key-concept — includes within its sweep the worlds of nature and of culture alike. The latter is denied not merely as a value. For the theistic world-view also devalues the world on account of its evanescence. The absolutist denies it as a real given. Lapse of value means lapse of reality. As one of the Hindu classics puts it, 'the snake is false at the very place and in the very moment that it appeared, substituting as it did, demonically, for the rope'.

One of the outcomes of this attitude, of great consequence for Hindu thought and life as a whole, is to view reality not horizontally but as a pyramid of levels succeeding each other in a vertical direction, according to their degree of value and of their consequent power of being. The world's encountered diversities and pluralities, its change, all that goes with freedom and action are all alike 'levelled' as belonging together under a common verdict. Unity, however, stands on a 'higher' level not contradicted by but contradicting diversity, so that movement is possible from below to above but not *vice versa*. 'From death to immortality' is the pattern. Not the other way round. Again, in the asymmetrical movement from one level to another, there is no organic transition implied in so far as the higher does not literally 'fulfil' the lower. *Telos* or fulfilment does not have a horizontal sense of lying at the end of the road. It is vertical, involving an 'ascent' or leap. 'Liberation', comparable to waking up from a dream, is an essential possibility present for man always, and at no time in particular. It is not, strictly, accomplishing something. Indeed, it is waking up from the illusion of accomplishment.

The model of 'waking from dream' likewise contains implicit answers to the problems of individuality, community or social obligation. When I 'wake up' from a dream I realize that all the individuals I saw in the dream were 'false', but I also realize that the person I call myself, with the body and behaviour I had in the dream, was equally 'false'. There is illusion, there is freedom from illusion, but individuals are not freed from illusion. Individuals are the products of illusion. Individuality is itself precisely the illusion from which we seek to be freed. You and I differ in our bodies, in the minds and egos associated with bodies, but we do not differ in self. It is by falsely identifying the self with the body that we suffer the illusion of individuality. The self is in the world as the sleeper is in his dream-world ; he is not really in it, he only seems to be. Similarly, the ethical problem simply does not arise for the 'liberated'. While dreaming, the dreamer has moral obligations to the persons in the dream. But after he wakes up from his dream he feels no obligation to go back to sleep in order to recover his dream and help those persons further, because he knows that they no longer exist — in fact they never did exist.

I have dwelt at some length on the absolutist's uncompromising views only to set off negatively the Hindu theist's frame of reference. Theistic Hinduism of all shades stands defined by its repudiation of the theory of falsity, and of the distinction of levels implied by it. In effect it may be said to affirm freedom, love, personality, community, history and moral obligation, and to rediscover their deeper spiritual significance for man. Their positive role in the service of man's freedom from the thraldom of unfreedom can be duly appreciated once man is 'liberated' from the penumbra of falsity. There is a spiritual purpose in history : to reclaim man estranged from himself and from others in consequence of his estrangement from the ground of his very being. God's cosmic functions are, to generalize the theology of Hindu theism, to help us to grow into full spiritual manhood. History as the sphere of man's conscious, deliberate and collective striving is what makes possible the realization of his values, though this is not itself viewed as 'accomplishment' but as an aspect of cosmic history.

Two kinds of eschatologies — under the categories of 'bondage' and 'liberation' — are used. In contrast to the generality of absolutistic thought, theism is sensitive of the continuity between the two. Bondage, or *samsara*, includes the conception of an 'after-life' which remains on the same level as the present life, and though comprising all forms of life, sub-human and super-human alike, is typified in regard to moral responsibility uniquely by human life. The corollary to this 'after-life' concept is *karma*. The individual continues from life to life in an embodied existence, the contents and forms of his life dependent on what the individual has performed in former lives, yet affording some scope for growth and gradual perfection by the performance of meritorious actions. This is the sphere of *dharma*.

The second eschatology consists of the assumption of a 'liberation' (*moksha*), from bondage into unending embodied existence. Negatively, it is the de-conditioning of the individual, subject to multiple conditionings or bonds; positively, it is unhindered conformity to the gracious will of God, not in spite of but in due compliance with the individual's freedom, and a consequent experience of blessedness in the wake of fulfilment and freedom.

Cosmic action on the part of the divine will is conceived imaginatively to consist of two phases. The initial phase involves the self-veiling of God, even while He is witness to the obstructing function of human ignorance. God is thus not only the ground but the hidden meaning and motive of history. The endless sequence of life and death, of wakefulness and sleep, of memory and oblivion, of creation and destruction, is really the grand work of God's construction, in free complicity with man obstructed in his vision and constricted in his action. History is not a series of meaningless recurrences of the 'natural' world but a process pointing and moving toward a fuller disclosure and realization of life's essential meaning. That this is so becomes apparent retrospectively in the experience of *moksha*. This marks the second phase of God's cosmic function. This is the self-revelation of God coinciding with the termination of bondage, which is of the nature of revelation. The entire sweep of man's existence thus stands in relation to God and as a preparation for *moksha*. No special religious sphere need be set apart from the secular world. Ordinary life as such takes on religious meaning. *Dharma* and *moksha* are continuous, the continuity of course being perceptible only from the perspective of the second.

It is also to be noted here that though bondage and liberation from bondage are alike 'caused' for man from without man, the decision however rests with man and depends on his preparation. Full scope is thus provided for man's being motivated to exert himself individually and collectively toward the common goal of liberation.

The essence of Hindu religiosity is often thought to be the immanent conception of Truth. Truth is something which cannot be introduced from without in time but is within the individual. The individual's task is accordingly to strive to appropriate the God within. This is the 'infinite resignation' of the ascetic who renounces the temporal for the sake of the eternal. Even the teacher cannot directly teach but only serve as a stimulus or occasion for the individual to help himself. He can, to use Socrates' words, stimulate but not 'beget'.

This view can, however, bear reassessment and reconstruction in the light of the reoriented understanding of the problem in Hindu theism, which conceives the individual to be transcendentally conditioned, as the being primordially divided from the truth by an infinite qualitative gulf. He neither has the truth nor is he able to acquire it. The teacher must supply the condition as well as the truth. This particular teacher can only be God. He acts in history, confronting man as the 'thou', exemplifying personal relationship and investing time with decisive significance. His action gives the temporal eternal significance. Man, tied to the temporal, is redeemed in time, 'at the appropriate moment' which is filled with the significance of the eternal.

Lastly, *moksha*, contrary to the belief that it cries halt to all dynamism, may be interpreted with the support of the authentic theistic tradition as implying the eternal conquest of the negative. *Eternal* blessedness involves the presence of three factors : the 'giver' and the 'enjoyer' and the 'occasioner'. By 'occasioner' is meant the negative factor which also paradoxically contributes to and even constitutes the experience of Blessedness. An example may be useful. Light dispels darkness. But does the latter become nonexistent ? When the light is withdrawn the darkness returns. This shows that darkness continues to exist even in the presence of the light. The latter continuously prevails against the continuously existent darkness by continuously dispelling it. Bondage is 'privation' of one's will, a thwarting of compliance with one's own unrestrained will which fulfils itself by conforming to Divine will. Liberation is a privation of this privation, a thwarting of the thwarting of will or, positively, a free unhampered exercise of will as in 'Thy will be done', which is joy itself. Even after attaining to the highest, life receives its content by 'repetition' or forward recollection. As Augustine says, commenting on the Psalm 'Seek His Face ever more', 'Finding should not end that seeking by which love is testified but with the increase of love, the seeking of the found one should also increase.'

III

The basic polarity which colours the meaning of *moksha* is the polarity of its negative and positive aspects. Liberation is liberation from pain, suffering and loss. From estrangement of every kind. From the dubious and vulnerable character of human existence. Yet for the precise theistic sense, one must also look into its positive aspect. It is liberation or freedom *to do*. The free man, religiously speaking, is one who is unhindered in his freedom of volitional conformity or coincidence with the Divine. It is the freedom of enjoying union with God. Freedom to enjoy is another way of saying freedom from any sort of engagement or impediment that stands in the way of fulfilling one's will to enjoy. It is freedom from impediments of both commission and omission. Again, the expression 'free from' suggests that one is happy and *relieved* to be without those things one is freed from. A set of circumstances become constraining only when one wants to do something that these circumstances prevent. The world is a bondage to the extent that the circumstances of worldly existence hinder the accomplishment of the desire for freedom to enjoy. Without the implication of will to enjoy we should hardly know the meaning of freedom. Bondage is a thwarting of one's will and liberation is a thwarting of bondage. The liberating agent merely arrests the arresting of the constraint or opposes its opposing.

The second polarity of meaning that gives substance to the theistic understanding of *moksha* is the polarity of the divine and the human. The factors involved are Divine grace and human freedom. Acknowledging either without the other leads to the partial emphasis of *moksha* as a prize to be won by one's efforts or as a gift freely given but not earned. This conflict runs through the entire Indian culture and is present in the West too, in the form of opposition between grace and self-reliance.

Grace supplies the essential transcendent element but it does not present itself as a total stranger ; rather as a welcome guest whose appearance was not only awaited but intensively aspired or craved with the whole of our centred self.

Theistic Hinduism affirms the paradox that in affirming God man affirms his selfhood. It is genuine self-affirmation rather than self-negation that is entailed by God-affirmation. Saving knowledge is of the form of overcoming of alienation. One becomes aware of the sense of alienation, of being lost to oneself and consequently to the world, paradoxically, in the God-consciousness which at the same time involves the overcoming of this alienation.

To acknowledge a polar relation between self-effort and grace as a feature characteristic of *moksha* enables the avoidance of the extremes of moral legalism and graceless moralism on the one side and amoral lawlessness and a supra-ethical mysticism on the other. It is the affirmation of moral conscience but as having a more than moral foundation. Being precedes action in everything that is, including man, although in man as the bearer of freedom previous action determines present being. *Moksha*, therefore, phenomenologically at least, understood strictly from the self-restricted perspective of the striving seeker, is not exclusively God's work utterly apart from man's latent resources and endowment. The latter must be utilized, transformed and transmuted. God must accept us if we are to accept God. This is not so much an external necessity placed upon God as the inner logic of the situation in which man stands before God, the situation presupposed by the distinction of bondage and freedom from bondage.

Hindu spirituality is thus able to appreciate the theme of how God's 'forgiveness' concretely comes to the fore, because it itself acknowledges Divine initiative in the sphere of knowledge and being, an initiative which does not contradict human freedom but rather assumes it and builds upon it. Hindus will simply add that man's real freedom to be himself comes by the surrender of all claims to isolated independence and self-willedness. Precisely this is what man contributes to his own deliverance which he must 'work out by fear and trembling', for the very reason that 'deliverance' belongs to God. We become aware that this is so in so far as we make ourselves open to the power of God which God makes available to us. Accepting God's acceptance of us, love answering love — this is also the profound theme of Hindu theism. *This* is liberation. Overcoming of suffering, escaping the round of rebirth, all these are circumstantial to it.

The words of Irenaeus about Christ 'as God becoming what we are that he might make us what he himself is' is also exactly the note of praise and prayer addressed by the pupil to his spiritual Master :

'I have seen His mercy's feet
Seen His roseate Feet this earth hath trod
Seen Him, even I have known the Blessed one
Seen in grace He made me His.'

(*Thiruvacakam*, a Tamil classic)

I shall close by briefly referring to two other sets of polarities of meaning in respect of *moksha*, the polarity of means and end and the polarity of the individual and the universal. These are what makes *moksha* a *spiritual* experience ; in the secular world there can only be conflict between them. The concept of the spiritual involves the identity of means and end. This is the paradox of spiritual realization. Realization is eternal realization. The goal of spiritual life is also a kind of life — life eternal, life divine or life universal, call it by any name. It involves no change in the modes of existence or even in the behaviour of the 'liberated' man. What he has been doing with a sense of 'ought' he now does spontaneously. The example that is given is significant. Milk is taken by the convalescent as a means for nourishment, and also by the healthy for conserving health. *Moksha* is also an eternal conservation of spiritual value, and is continuous with its means. Conversely, knowledge, work, devotion are all involved in the accomplished character of *moksha*. The dawn of saving faith is itself in principle coincident with the advent of *moksha*.

The polarity is also exemplified by the equation of Revelation with liberation. The history of Divine self-disclosure and the 'history' of man's liberation from bondage are one and the same history. The bestowal of revelatory grace is *moksha*, just as the veiling of it is bondage. Lastly, 'liberation' does not imply fulfilment of the individual in isolation. A limited fulfilment of separate individuals would not be fulfilment at all, not even for the individuals, for no person is separated from other persons and from the whole of reality in such a way that he could be 'liberated' apart from the liberation of everyone and everything. This is the polarity of individual and universal.

This demand is implicitly present in classical Hinduism and becomes explicitly articulated in medieval and modern Hinduism, thus giving a religious urgency to community and institutional life. *Moksha* is conceived as an 'empire' where one's autonomy is truly regained. It is an empire of emperors in complete possession of their empire which is only to say : of themselves in conscious conformity with God. There is complete transparency of everything for the divine to shine through, so that there is no tension of claim and counterclaim. Just as *moksha* may be conceived as life that finally triumphs over what restricts it (death), it can also be viewed as a Divine universe or kingdom, triumphing over the demonic power structure that is the world.

In this paper, I have purposefully highlighted those areas of interest in connection with a discussion on the meaning of *moksha* that will be of significance for dialogue between Hindu and Christian religions. Even at the risk of a certain measure of oversimplification and blurring of distinctions, to which charge I shall plead guilty, I have striven to indicate certain structural affinities between the ideas of 'Salvation in history' and 'Liberation from bondage'. The convergences and divergences which follow should provide the grist for fruitful dialogue.

BUDDHIST *NIRVANA* : ITS SIGNIFICANCE IN CONTEMPORARY THOUGHT AND LIFE

MASAO ABE [1]

I

Nirvana is often misunderstood in the West as being something negative. This misunderstanding sometimes occurs even in the Buddhist world, for the literal meaning of *nirvana* is the extinction or annihilation of passion, often compared to the extinguishing of a fire. But is *nirvana* negative ? What is the real meaning of *nirvana*?

The fundamental teaching of Gautama the Buddha (the founder of Buddhism), the Four Holy Truths, is as follows : that existence is suffering ; that the cause of suffering is craving or habitual thirst ; that by the extinction of craving, existence may attain *nirvana ;* and that the means for the attainment of *nirvana* is the practice of the Eightfold Holy Path : right view, right intention, right speech, right conduct, right livelihood, right effort, right mindfulness, and right concentration.

When Gautama the Buddha says 'existence is (characterized by) suffering' he does not mean that human life is simply full of suffering without any pleasure at all. It is obvious that there is pleasure as well as suffering in human life. In daily life we distinguish between pleasure and suffering, seeking for and clinging to pleasure while avoiding and detesting suffering. This is inherent in human nature. However, according toBuddhism, real suffering (henceforth referred to as Suffering with a capital 'S') lies in this very inclination. Pleasure and suffering are in reality inseparable — one is never found without the other — and the position that they are rigidly separable is abstract and unreal. Therefore, the more we try to cling to pleasure and avoid suffering, the more entangled we become in the duality of pleasure and suffering. It is this whole process which constitutes Suffering. When Gautama the Buddha says 'existence is (characterized by) suffering', he is referring to this Suffering and not suffering as opposed to pleasure. It is the reality of this non-relative Suffering which man can realize at the existential ground which lies deep within himself beneath the duality of pleasure and suffering. Since life and death are the fundamental sources of pleasure and suffering, human existence is

[1] Professor ABE, a Zen Buddhist, is a professor at the Nara University of Education, Kyoto, Japan.

understood in Buddhism to be irrevocably bound to *samsara*, the cycle of birth and death.

Accordingly, when Gautama the Buddha says 'the cause of suffering is craving', he means by craving not simply the attachment to pleasure but a deeper and more fundamental attachment that is rooted in human existence, that of loving pleasure and hating suffering, with its accompanying phenomenon of making a distinction between the two. According to Gautama's teaching, this fundamental attachment originates in an illusory view of life in the world which is the result of basic ignorance innate in human nature. Craving is a human passion linked to man's entanglement in the duality of pleasure and suffering, and deeply rooted in the ego. It is by extinguishing this craving that *nirvana* can be attained. Thus *nirvana* is not a *negative* or *lifeless state* such as the mere annihilation of human passion would suggest, but an *existential awakening* to egolessness, *anatta* or *anatman*, attained through liberation from craving, the attachment to the dualistic view which distinguishes between pleasure as something to be sought after and suffering to be avoided.

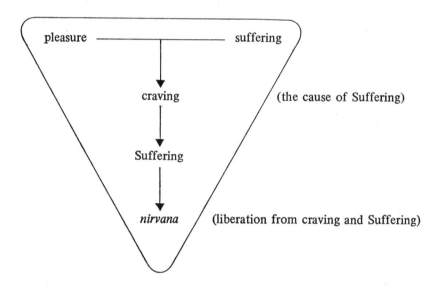

The position of Gautama the Buddha can be clearly seen in his first sermon after his enlightenment :

Monks, these two extremes should not be followed by one who has gone forth as a wanderer. What two ?

Wingate College Library

Devotion to the pleasure of sense, a low practice of villagers, a practice unworthy, unprofitable, the way of the world (on the one hand); and (on the other) devotion to self-mortification, which is painful, unworthy and unprofitable.

By avoiding these two extremes the *Tathagata* (the Buddha) has gained knowledge of that Middle Path which giveth vision, which giveth knowledge, which causes calm, special knowledge, enlightenment, *nirvana*.[2]

In this connection, the following four points are to be noted:

1) Gautama the Buddha takes the Middle Way, transcending both hedonism and asceticism. Accordingly, he does not negate human desire as such but, in avoiding these two extremes, relegates it to its proper position in human life. However, the Middle Way is not simply a midpoint between pleasure and suffering, but rather is the Way which *transcends* the very duality of pleasure and suffering. Thus living the Middle Way is none other than being in *nirvana*.

2) For Buddhism, the Middle Way or *nirvana* is not an objectively observable state nor something which can be considered a goal of life, but rather an existential ground from which human life can properly begin without becoming entangled in the duality of pleasure and suffering. By living the Middle Way, in *nirvana*, we can be master of, and not slave to, pleasure and suffering. In this sense, *nirvana* is the source of human freedom and creative activity.

3) In his awakening to egolessness, Gautama the Buddha transcended not only the particular duality of pleasure and suffering, but duality itself. In other words, he could awaken to egolessness only when he came to be freed from duality itself, and this he achieved through overcoming the particular duality of pleasure and suffering. Accordingly, *nirvana* as the existential awakening to egolessness is beyond any kind of duality, including that of good and evil, right and wrong, life and death, man and nature, and even that of man and God. To attain *nirvana* in this sense is, for Buddhism, salvation.

4) Although *nirvana*, or the Middle Way, is beyond duality, it is not characterized by a monistic view. Monism is not yet free from duality, for it is still opposed to dualism or pluralism. Being beyond duality, the view of one who has attained *nirvana* is not monistic but rather nondualistic. This is why Buddhism does not proclaim only one God, but speaks of *Sunyata* (Emptiness). Emptiness is realized by going beyond

---

[2] *The Book of the Kindred Sayings*, Part V. Translated by F. L. Woodward. Luzac for the Pali Text Society, 1930, p. 356.

one God and thus is not the relative emptiness of a mere vacuum. Being beyond one God, Emptiness is identical to, or, more strictly speaking, 'non-dualistic' with respect to individual things, making them truly individual. Indeed, in Emptiness, all is all in the sense that all is as it is and *at the same time* all is equal in its as-it-is-ness. The following question-and-answer dialogue between the Chinese Zen master, Jōshu (778-897), and a monk illustrates the point. The monk asked Jōshu, 'All things are reduced to the One; where is this One to be reduced to?' Jōshu replied, 'When I was in the province of Tsin I had a monk's robe made that weighed seven pounds.'[3] That which is ultimate or universal is not the One to which all things are reducible but a particular thing, absolutely irreplaceable, such as a monk's robe, which has a particular weight and is made at a particular place at a particular time. The universal and a particular thing are paradoxically one in the realization of Emptiness, which goes beyond the understanding which sees all things as reducible to One.

Oneness as a universal principle, if substantial and self-existing, must be overcome; otherwise we as particulars lose our individuality and cannot possibly awaken to Reality. From the Buddhist point of view, this is true even for God, the only One. On the other hand, if all particular things are respectively self-identical, there is no equality between them and everything is self-centred. Both Emptiness, the negation of Oneness, and egolessness, the negation of everything's self-centredness, are necessary for awakening. In the realization of Emptiness, which is another term for *nirvana*, all particular things are respectively just as they are and equal in their suchness. This is expressed in Mahayana Buddhism as 'difference as it is, is sameness; sameness (of things in their suchness) as it is, is difference'. This very realization is the source of wisdom and compassion in which both ignorance and self-centredness are overcome. Just because *nirvana* is in itself empty, it is full of particular things functioning freely, neither losing their particularity nor impeding each other.

II

What significance does Buddhist *nirvana* hold for us today, East or West, in contemporary thought and life, especially in regard to the problems of understanding ultimate reality, nihilism, the relation of

---

[3] *Pi-yen chi* (The Blue Cliff Collection), Case 45. See also Suzuki, D. T.: *Introduction to Zen Buddhism.* Rider & Co., p. 72.

nature and man's personality, the irrational in human existence, achieving true community, and understanding the meaning of history ? I would like to deal with these problems from the viewpoint of Mahayana Buddhism, a form of Buddhism developed in northern Asia, especially in China and Japan, and based on a dynamic interpretation of Gautama's teaching. First of all, *nirvana* has relevance to man's understanding of ultimate or universal reality in that it overcomes the major objection to monistic absolutism. The concept of one God who is essentially transcendent, self-existing apart from everything relative, is illusory to Buddhism in that He cannot be spoken or without a knower. In Buddhism, mutual relativity is the ultimate truth, and doctrines of absolute truth which exclude other views of truth as false are similarly considered illusory. In *nirvana*, nothing is independent, self-existing, or permanent ; having no permanent selfhood, everything is mutually related to each and every other thing. This is not a fixed relativism simply rejecting absolutes and resulting in a form of scepticism or nihilism, but a dynamic relativism in which even the absolute and the relative, the holy and the secular, the divine and the human, are all totally interrelated. This idea of the total interrelatedness of each and everything at every moment is also termed 'dependent co-origination' in Buddhism, the realization of which is none other than *nirvana*. Dynamic relativism, being beyond the opposition between relativism and absolutism, is at once dynamic absolutism. This paradoxical truth can be realized not through speculation but only through existential practice (e.g., the practice of the Eightfold Holy Path, and Buddhist sitting meditation).

The position of Buddhism toward other faiths is often called 'tolerant' by Western scholars. However, it may be that the term 'tolerant' has been applied according to Western, especially Christian, standards, and is misleading in that it does not get to the heart of Buddhism. The Buddhist position, founded in *nirvana*, is a 'positionless position' in the sense that, being itself empty, it lets every other position stand and work just as it is. Naturally, Buddhism does not exclude other faiths as false, but recognizes the relative truths which they contain. This recognition, however, is a starting point, not an end, for Buddhist life. Properly speaking, Buddhism starts to work critically and creatively *through* this basic recognition of the relative truths contained in other positions, hoping for productive dialogue and cooperation with other faiths.

This Buddhist position realized in *nirvana* may prove effective in a contemporary world which is seeing a remarkable rise of a sense of the diversity of values as it becomes more and more closely united. The dynamic relativism of *nirvana* may provide a spiritual foundation for the formation of the rapidly approaching One World in which the co-existence of a variety of contrasting values and ways of life is indispensable.

Secondly, *nirvana* offers a freedom beyond nihilism. One of the serious problems in the world today is the permeation of nihilism such as was proclaimed by Friedrich Nietzsche. The collapse of traditional value systems and a cry of 'God is dead' are somewhat universal phenomena in industrialized societies. A loss of the sense of the holy and despair of established forms of religion prevail in the world today. It has become more and more difficult for modern man to believe in 'God' with the pervasion of the scientific way of thinking; yet people today are searching seriously for something to fill the vacuum which has been created in their spiritual lives. In this respect, Nietzsche is a touchstone for religion, for he advocated as a prototype of future man the active nihilist who, being based on the Will of Power, courageously faces emptiness without God. However, it is unlikely that Nietzsche's active nihilism can successfully serve as a substitute for religion. It would seem that what is needed today and in the future is a religion beyond active nihilism, i.e. a religion beyond 'emptiness without God'. Buddhism, which is based on *nirvana*, is precisely a religion of this sort. Negating the existence of one God, Buddhism advocates *Sunyata* (Emptiness) which is not a nihilistic emptiness but rather a fulness of particular things and individual men functioning fully and without hindrance. In Emptiness, everything is realized as it *is*, in its total dynamic reality. This radical realism involves not only liberation from 'God' but also the overcoming of an active nihilism such as advocated by Nietzsche.[4]

Nirvana is a realization of great freedom, both from theistic pietism with its dependence on God and from nihilism with its dependence on the Will to Power, making possible self-determination by removing the illusion of a determinator.

Thirdly, *nirvana* has relevance to our understanding of the relation of nature and man's personality. Christian scholars often complain that Buddhist *nirvana* is impersonal. Christian personalism, if I am not mistaken, is based on man's responsibility to the Word of God. Unlike other creatures, man is created in God's image and can respond to the calling

---

[4] ABE, MASAO: 'Christianity and Buddhism Centering Around Science and Nihilism', *Japanese Religions*. Kyoto: NCC Study Centre, Vol. 5, No. 3.

of God. Nature is ruled by God through man whom God gave 'dominion over' other creatures. In this sense, Christian personalism is connected with anthropocentrism. Contrary to this, Buddhist *nirvana* is based on egolessness and is not anthropocentric but rather cosmological. In Buddhism, man and nature are equally subject to change, transitory and transmigratory. Man cannot achieve emancipation from the cycle of birth and death until he can eliminate a more universal problem — the transience common to all things in the universe. Here we see that the *basis* for Buddhist salvation is cosmological, not personalistic as in terms of an I-Thou relationship with God, and thus impersonal and trans-anthropocentric. However, it is only *man* with his self-consciousness and free will who can go beyond anthropocentrism and reach an awareness that transience is not limited to man but is common to all things. Furthermore, it is noteworthy that Buddhist salvation is primarily concerned with individual persons, not necessarily man in general, for, as is written in a Scripture, 'One is born alone, dies alone, comes alone, and goes alone.' [5] In this sense Buddhism may also be said to be personalistic and existentialistic. Yet this does not mean that man is understood in Buddhism in terms of a divine-human encounter in which nature is excluded, but rather that man is understood as a being with self-consciousness and free will on a cosmological basis which includes all of nature. Without the realization of transience and selflessness on such a cosmological basis, a person cannot become an 'awakened one'.[6]

Here we see the following two aspects of Buddhist salvation : 1) Buddhism is primarily concerned with the salvation of man as a person who, unlike other living beings, has self-consciousness and free will and thereby alone has the potential to become awakened to and emancipated from the transience common to all things in the universe. This is the existentialistic and personalistic aspect of Buddhism. However, 2) a cosmological dimension is the necessary *basis* for this Buddhist salvation because the salvation of man is in Buddhism not salvation from sin as rebellion against God, but emancipation from the cycle of birth and death which is part of the transience of the universe. This is the cosmological aspect of Buddhism. These two aspects are inseparable — the more cosmological the basis is, the more existential the salvation is. In this sense, the

---

[5] *The Larger Sukhavati-vyuha.*
[6] ABE, MASAO: 'Man and Nature in Christianity and Buddhism', *Japanese Religions*, Vol. 7, No. 1.

Buddhist cosmology which is the basis of *nirvana* is an existential cosmology and Buddhist existentialism or personalism may be called 'cosmo-existentialism' or 'cosmo-personalism'.[7]

The Buddhist position with regard to the relation of man and nature may contribute a spiritual foundation toward the solution of a pressing problem that man is faced with today — destruction of the environment coupled with estrangement from nature. This problem is a result of man's anthropocentrism whereby he regards nature merely as a means or obstacle to the realization of his own selfish goals, and thus continually finds ways to utilize and conquer it. On the other hand, the cosmological view which is the basis of Buddhist *nirvana* does not see nature as something subordinate to man, but sees man as subordinate to nature, more precisely as a part of nature from the standpoint of 'cosmos'. Thus the cosmological view both allows man to overcome his estrangement from nature and to live harmoniously with nature without losing his individuality.

Fourthly, let us consider what significance Buddhist *nirvana* may have in dealing with the irrational in human existence. Interest in mythology and primitive cultures as well as an irresistible demand to release instinctive, especially sexual, desire is on the upsurge in highly industrialized societies. This phenomenon may be regarded as a reaction to the emphasis on human rationality and science which grew up in modern European culture and formed the basis for industrialization. Western thinkers such as Schopenhauer, Marx, Freud and Jung, and, more recently, Camus, Marcuse and others emphasize in various ways the importance of the irrational aspects of human existence. Another important problem of human existence which modern European culture has completely neglected is the problem of death, for modern man the supreme irrationality.

In short, modern European culture with its scientific orientation, pervasive as it is in highly industrialized societies, is based on human rationality and the principle of life, while neglecting to deal with the irrational elements in human existence, especially death. However, it may not be wise for us simply to accept and follow present reactionary tendencies to this emphasis on rationalism. What is necessary today in order to deal successfully with this problem is a profound basis upon which the

[7] ABE, MASAO: 'Dogen on Buddha Nature', *The Eastern Buddhist*, Vol. IV, No. 1, Kyoto: Eastern Buddhist Society, Otani University.

conflicts between the rational and the irrational, reason and desire, or life and death, can be resolved. Buddhist *nirvana*, or the Middle Way, in which man overcomes duality and extinguishes the 'craving' deeply rooted in human existence, may provide such a basis.

Fifthly, let us consider what significance Buddhist *nirvana* may have in the understanding and achievement of true community. It is the realization of *nirvana*, quoted previously, that 'difference as it is, is sameness ; sameness as it is, is difference' which, for Buddhism, provides an existential ground for true community. We find ourselves equal, not as children of one God, but in the common realization of egolessness or Emptiness, which is at the same time the realization of true Self. Realization of egolessness is not something negative, like losing one's self-identity, but is positive in the sense that through it one overcomes one's ego-centredness and awakens to Reality, that is, to one's own true Self as well as the true Self of others. It is in this awakening that one can live with others in true community, sharing the realization of true Self. In *nirvana*, the loss of ego-self is the gain of true Self, and the sameness among individuals in their egolessness and the difference between individuals in their true Self-ness are paradoxically one.

Accordingly, in the realization of *nirvana*, I am not I because I am egoless, and yet I am absolulety I because I am my true Self. Likewise, you are not you because you are egoless, and yet you are absolutely you because you are your true Self. Moreover, since I am not I, I am you, and since you are not you, you are I. Each person remains just as he is, yet each person is identical in being his true Self. This dynamic interrelationship occurs in the common realization of egolessness and Emptiness. This realization provides the Buddhist foundation for man in true community. Furthermore, this realization applies not only to man's relationship to man, but to all things in nature, from dogs to mountains.

Sixth and finally, what significance does *nirvana* have in regard to understanding the meaning of history ? Since there is no God in Buddhism, there is no Creation or Last Judgment, but rather Emptiness. Thus, for Buddhism, history has neither beginning nor end. This view of history derives from the deep realization of the *karma* of human beings. *Karma* is the universal law of act and consequence which is self-operating in making the self transform unceasingly from one life to another and the world a process of perpetual becoming. Thus it is action-energy which produces various effects according to the nature of the action and which binds men to the wheel of birth and death. Unlike the Hindu concept of *karma*, however, *karma* in Buddhism is not deterministic since there is in Buddhism no idea of God who is the controller of *karma*; rather, Buddhism takes *karma* as moral energy, emphasizing the possibility of man's final release from the round of transmigration through the exercising of his free will. Accordingly, on the one hand, we are bound by our own *karma* which shares in and is inseparably linked to *karma* operating in the universe but, on the other hand, we, as beings with self-consciousness and free will, have the opportunity to be liberated from *karma* through our own free act, an act which is based on the total realization within oneself of the beginningless and endless process of *karma*, i.e. *karma* operating in the universe beyond oneself. In this total realization of *karma*, personal and universal, past, present and future, one is liberated from *karma* and awakens to *nirvana*.

At the very moment we truly realize the beginninglessness and endlessness of history, we transcend its boundlessness and find the whole process of history from beginningless beginning to endless end intensively concentrated within the here and now. Apart from the moment of realization, there is no history. We realize our true life and true Self at this moment in which beginning and end, time and eternity, and one and all are not seen in duality but in dynamic oneness. This is nothing other than the realization of *nirvana*.

Universal *karma* can be realized not objectively but only subjectively, i.e. in and through the existential realization of personal and individual *karma* — and personal *karma* can be truly transcended only when universal *karma* is subjectively overcome within oneself. Thus (1) *to one who has attained nirvana* through the total realization of *karma*, the whole universe discloses itself in its reality and history as the endless process of operating *karma* ceases, eternity manifesting itself. In this sense history ends in *nirvana*. This is the universal salvation of *nirvana* realized by an awakened one, and represents the wisdom aspect of *nirvana*. At the same time, however, (2) *for the awakened one* history begins in *nirvana* because those who, despite *the fact of* universal salvation realized by an awakened one, *think themselves* to be 'unsaved', remain innumerably in the world and will appear endlessly in the future. Thus history has a new leaning for an awakened one — it is an endless process in which he must try to actualize universal salvation in regard to those 'unsaved'. This represents the compassion aspect of *nirvana*. Since the wisdom and compassion aspects are inseparable in *nirvana*, history begins and ends at each moment in the realization of *nirvana*.

In short, for an awakened one who is living *nirvana*, universal salvation is completely realized in the here and now, and yet it is to be realized endlessly in the process of history by those who *think themselves* to be 'unsaved'. These two aspects are dynamically united in *nirvana*. Accordingly, at each and every moment of history a development toward the endless future is at once a total return to the root and source of history, i.e. eternity, and *vice versa*, where history is a succession of such moments. This Buddhist view of history leads us to a double realization: in the light of wisdom eternity manifests itself in the here and now, and the present life is not a means to a future end, but is the end itself, while in the light of compassion life is an endless activity of saving others, an instrument for universal salvation.

REDEMPTION: A CONTEMPORARY JEWISH UNDERSTANDING

ZVI YARON [1]

Redemption has always been one of the significant tenets of Judaism. From biblical times to our own age the idea of *ge'ula*, redemption, had a remarkable influence upon Jewish theology and the texture of Jewish life. Over the centuries its meaning underwent many changes, but its persistently focal role in Jewish life is attested by its pervasive dominance in the daily liturgy. There are prayers for redemption and there are benedictions in which God is praised as the redeemer of Israel. There are anxious prayers for deliverance from affliction and stress, and there are expressions of confident hope and even assurance that the redemption will be fulfilled.

The exodus from Egypt is both starting point and prototype for the future redemption. The exodus is mentioned in the prayers and in the *kiddush*, the consecration of the Sabbath and the festivals. The memory of the past exodus is intended to turn the exodus into an active contemporary event which has profound implications for the nature of the relationship between the people of Israel and God. The past redemptive event is absorbed in the consciousness of the people. The contents and the quality of Jewish life are thus shaped by an event which although it took place in antiquity continues to exercise a dynamic influence upon the people. This influence is persistently effective because each generation consciously imbibes the long-ago event. This is expressed in one of the most important ceremonies of the Jewish year, the festive service on the first evening of the Passover festival. This service is entitled *seder*, for it is conducted according to a traditional 'order' which includes the narration *(haggada)* of the exodus in wide-ranging interpretations. The aim of the *haggada* is tersely stated in a declarative sentence:

> In every single generation it is a man's duty to regard himself as if he came out of Egypt. As it is said in the Bible, 'And thou shalt tell thy son on that day, saying: This is because of what God did to me when I came out of Egypt' (Exodus 13:8).

[1] Dr YARON is director of the Public Relations and Press Department of the Jewish Agency and teaches on religious and cultural life in Israel in the Department for Overseas Students, Hebrew University, Jerusalem.

> For it is not only our fathers whom the Holy One (blessed be He) redeemed; but we were also redeemed with them.
> As it is said in the Bible,
> 'And He brought us out of there, that He might bring us in, to give us the land of which He swore to our fathers' (Deuteronomy, 6 : 23).

Throughout a long and varied history the idea of redemption has always had both physical and spiritual meanings. These manifold interpretations of ge'ula have their origin in the sixth chapter of Exodus. God's promise of redemption includes the idea of the covenant between God and Israel, the deliverance from slavery and affliction, the pledge to lead the people to the promised land, and the theological implication of the redemption : 'And I will take you to Me for a people and I will be to you a God, and ye shall know that I am the Lord your God' (Exodus 6 : 7).

The various seemingly contradictory aspects are intertwined into a comprehensive view of redemption. They are not seen as opposed types of redemption but as possibilities which may be fully developed side by side or on different levels of apprehension. Thus the physical exodus is not contrasted with the spiritual meaning of divine redemption. Rather, the physical acquires a more profound and lasting meaning through the emphasis upon the spiritual. There are times when a particular aspect of redemption is emphasized. But in all circumstances and in all periods the idea of redemption never entirely loses its meaning of a total ge'ula which embraces all facets of human life.

Equally, there are nuances of emphasis on the question of whether redemption is conditional upon repentance. The Bible has given rise to various possibilities. For instance, in Deuteronomy (30 : 1-3) the repentance of the people precedes the redemption. First the people returns to God and then God redeems them. But there is also the other possibility, that God redeems the people when they are still steeped in sin, as it is reflected in chapter 36 of Ezekiel. Throughout Jewish history both possibilities were held up side by side, and they were thus integrated into the visions and hopes for redemption, although emphasis shifted as circumstances changed.

The biblical ge'ula concept took on a different hue during the period of the Second Temple. But the most profound changes in the perception of ge'ula evolved after the destruction of the Temple and the loss of national independence in 70 C.E. The idea of ge'ula was always bound up with galut, the abnormal and temporary situation when the people is in exile. But since the year 70 a profound change affected the people of Israel. The roles of *ge'ula* and *galut* were reversed. A Jew in 1972 looking back at his nation's long history is struck by the fact that *galut*, exile, has been the norm of existence far longer than the comparatively very short periods of *ge'ula*. This overriding fact could have caused utter despair and despondency, but in Judaism the faith in the divine guiding of history gave rise to a constant search for the deeper meaning of exile. Whilst *galut* continued to mean physical and political exile, it also alluded to theological implications.

Since Jewish nationality has always had theological significance, the changes in the conditions of national existence assumed religious importance. The religiosity of Jewish nationality was summed up by Sa'adya Gaon, the tenth-century philosopher, in what came to be regarded as a classic dictum : 'Our nation, the Children of Israel, is a nation only by virtue of the Tora.' In the prologue to the Ten Commandments (Exodus 19 : 3-6) the Israelites are enjoined to be 'a kingdom of priests and a holy nation'. Commenting on this verse, Martin Buber pointed out that it involved not only the behaviour of individual members of the people, but the dedication to God of the nation, with all its substance and all its functions, with legal form and institutions, with the organization of its internal and external relationships. The corollary is that in Jewish theology the organized Jewish community, all its activities and its conditions of existence, have religious significance. As Abraham Heschel put it : 'For us Jews there can be no fellowship with the people of Israel. What we do as individuals is a trivial episode, what we attain as Israel causes us to grow into the infinite.'

Galut is therefore not only political and physical exile and dispersion, but also spiritual and religious exile. Jewish theology uses terminology which implies as it were that the 'divine presence' is in exile. As Gershom Scholem has pointed out, Jewish mysticism views the exile of the people of Israel as the concrete and cruel expression of the state-of-exile of the unredeemed world. Israel-in-exile reflects a spiritual situation which must be changed and remedied, and it is the task of the people of Israel to bring about the spiritual changes which will put an end to the state-of-exile. These changes can be made through a way of living which is devoted to God, the Tora and the fulfilment of the *mitsvot*, the divine commandments. *Galut* is not only the divine punishment for the people's sins. It reflects a spiritual situation and it implies that the people in exile is entrusted with the task to alter the situation and bring about the redemption, which will also be both physical and spiritual. The redemption will therefore come as the result of a long, arduous and gradual work of spiritual improvement. In the same way that *galut* expresses a spiritual state-of-exile, *ge'ula* will reflect the changed and remedied state of the spiritual life. In this theology of *galut* and *ge'ula* there is no dichotomy of the material and the spiritual. Both exile and redemption contain all the elements and facets of life, the political and physical being intertwined with the inner and the spiritual.

This all-embracing view of exile and redemption is an integral part of the essential Jewish teaching that there is no absolute bifurcation of the secular and the religious. The Jewish view of religion embodies the twin elements of prophecy and *halakha*, religious law. Prophetic tradition has lent to Judaism its passion, its preoccupation with human affairs, its determination to criticize social evils, to denounce abuses and corruption. The *halakha* on the other hand has furnished a discipline, a pattern of conduct, thus involving Judaism inextricably in human civilization. Prophecy imbued religious faith with a sense of dynamic tension, of dissatisfaction with the contemporary. *Halakha* gave it constancy and regularity. These dual influences, the dynamism of the prophetic urge and the regularity induced by the *halakha*, confer on Judaism its sensitive awareness of the here and now, of the human condition in our world, bringing heaven down to earth, because nothing mundane is alien to the holy. At the same time there is the constant urge to probe the inner and spiritual meaning of events and to relate them to the divine purpose.

Against this background of the religious integration of the whole of human life, the *galut* and *ge'ula* concepts stand out as central motifs of both material and spiritual elements in Jewish life. But the predominance of these motifs is not of a static nature. Exile and redemption reflect the continuous movement and the urge for change. Exile may last for centuries, but it is expressive of a situation which is bound to change. The 16th-century philosopher Rabbi Loew of Prague taught that exile was an unnatural, abnormal state for a people. The natural way of living was, he wrote, for a people to live independently and normally in its own country. And since exile and dispersion were not natural, it was inconceivable that they will last forever. We must regard *galut* as a situation which is bound to come to an end, sooner or later, to be replaced by *ge'ula*, the redemption of Israel which will herald the redemption of mankind. The dispersed parts of the people will then unite and they will no longer be subjugated by other nations. And although exile has lasted for so many centuries, the very term *galut* implies its abnormality. Even if it spans almost two thousand years, it is ephemeral in terms of the divine purpose in human existence. For *galut* is a concept which acquires its full meaning only when it is related to *ge'ula*. Exile is a situation which constantly points to redemption. But a profound change has come over the Jewish people during the last two centuries. Crises, both political and spiritual, were not new in Jewish history. But the series of crises which affected the Jewish people in modern times were cataclysmic, and they threatened its continued existence. This period opened with the lure of emancipation, when European nations held out for the Jews the promise of complete freedom at the price of the total obliteration of Jewish identity. At the end of this period, and in our own time, we witnessed the most frightful abomination when mankind stood silently by whilst the Nazis exterminated six million Jews. In between these two extremities the Jewish people experienced every imaginable kind of crisis. There were pogroms, Jews suffered economic chicanery, they were subjected to social discrimination, they lived under political disabilities, and were constantly exposed to antisemitic vilification. At the same time they participated in the modern soul-searching about the truths and values of religious faith. And throughout this general erosion of old beliefs, Jews grappled with their own traditional faith and pattern of living. The resulting differences in opinions, beliefs and behaviour were far more profound and extensive than any that had occurred earlier in history. If the challenges of modern secularism are unprecedented in the history of mankind, they are of crucial importance to the Jewish people. For no other people has been so closely involved and identified with religion. The nature of this identification was recently described by the Jewish historian Isaac Baer : 'Religion had a decisive influence on the history of Greece and Rome as well as on the mediaeval history of Europe. Yet there were in the political and literary history of other nations periods devoid of religion, when the nations removed these matters from the sway of religion. But in our history such non-religious areas were almost non-existent... until the close of the period of Enlightenment.'

Out of these numerous and uninterrupted crises which thoroughly shook the foundations of Judaism and Jewish existence, arose the Zionist movement with the declared aim to put an end to the abnormalcy of *galut* by redeeming the Jewish people and gathering the dispersed exiles in its homeland, *Eretz Yisrael*, the Land of Israel.

But Zionism is not only a thoroughgoing solution for the agonizing predicament of modern Jewish existence. It is a movement of renewal which is at once revolutionary in its immediate aim to normalize Jewish conditions — and conservative in its long-term goal to restore Israel's ancient independence and revive the Hebrew language and culture. Under the impact of Zionism the *galut* is no longer understood as merely abnormal and ephemeral. It is intolerable and it ought to be abolished. Zionism teaches that *ge'ula* is not only the final goal of history. It is an urgent necessity and it must be brought about without delay. And if the prolonged sufferings were not enough to underline the urgency of *ge'ula*, there came the horrible Nazi holocaust — in the midst of an advanced 20th century and in enlightened Europe — to give painful poignance to the gravity of the *galut* situation and the pressing need to act.

The State of Israel is therefore understood in the messianic terms of the abolition of *galut* and the beginning of *ge'ula*. It is viewed with the biblical perception of a 'great and terrible wonder'. The Jewish people, having survived persecution and hatred, has now carried through an unequalled national revival and demonstrated its unique resilience. Jews never despaired ; inspired by faith they daily prayed for redemption and they were confident that their prayers will be fulfilled. And now the return to Zion, the ingathering of the exiles, and the reclamation of the desolate homeland, are the manifestations of the process of *ge'ula* at work. What distinguishes the contemporary *ge'ula* is the sense of urgency and impatience which has moved the Zionist movement and the growth of the State of Israel.

This view of the contemporary events affecting the Jewish people, of the vicissitudes of persecution and holocaust and of the amazing revival and restoration, is rooted in the conviction that history is far more than a mere accumulation of successive happenings. Not only in the distant past was Jewish history unique, but this century, too, is pregnant with messianic indications. The Zionist movement, the existence of the Jewish State and the ingathering of the exiles in the State, are intimations of the unfolding and progressive redemption. This redemption is physical and political and down-to-earth. And yet, there is something great and mysterious and ineffable in the history of *galut* and in the contemporary unfolding of *ge'ula*. Jews differ today about the nature and meaning of this mystery. Some speak of God and revelation, whilst others prefer to describe it as 'spirit'. But most Jews have experienced each momentous event in our time as if it were a stroke of a hammer, and the sequence of gruesome misery and painful tribulations were sensed in the biblical phrase of being hurled up and down and wound round and round (Isaiah 22 : 17). And the redemption, too, is sensed in the transcendent meaning of the messianic vision and the traditional idea of *ge'ula*.

The different views held today by Jews can probably be best exemplified by the two most prominent and influential Jews of our time, Mr David Ben-Gurion and Rabbi Abraham Isaac Kook. Ben-Gurion is world-renowned as the statesman who founded and led the State of Israel. And although he has through his life been a man of action, he has always been acutely conscious of the transcendent implications of the events in which he took a leading part. Rabbi Kook was the first chief rabbi of the Land of Israel (he died in 1935) and he is generally recognized as the greatest religious personality in Jewish life of recent times.

Ben-Gurion represents in his thinking the humanist-socialist trend in Zionism. And yet he shares with Rabbi Kook the view of Zionism as the unfolding process of *ge'ula*. With Kook it is mainly a theological interpretation, in which the Jewish people is fulfilling the task imposed by God, whilst to Ben-Gurion it is the people which carries its vision and presses forward to translate vision into reality. But this vision has a transcendent dimension. 'I accept the belief in God', Ben-Gurion writes in his *Biblical Reflections*, 'not as a belief in a corporeality, a God who ascends and descends and with whom people speak... For I accept Maimonides' view that God has no mouth and does not utter sounds, that he has no body and no physical shape.' Whilst affirming the humanistic character of ethics, Ben-Gurion declares his profound wonder at the ineffable. He is not a religious believer in the traditionally Jewish sense ; but he has a mystically-religious faith in the Bible as a mysterious work. His conception of Zionism is shaped by a mystical longing for the kind of 'normalcy' that is described in the Bible. The Jewish nation is not only a political entity, but embodies a moral will and carries a historical vision. The Jewish people has engaged in a 'stiffnecked' struggle not merely for physical survival but for its principles and beliefs.

Rabbi Kook was that rare twentieth-century phenomenon of the deeply religious mystic with a radically modern interest in human affairs. His view of Jewish nationality is the traditional postulate of its religious quality as a fact embodied in its long history. Kook phrases his thinking in mystical terms : 'The nature of the soul of the congregation of Israel is its divinity.' Quoting the Bible's consistent castigation of the people of Israel, he argues that the divine 'choice' of Israel was not a reward but a claim. The 'divine' character of its nationality is intended to spur the people to respond to the divine challenge. The religious quality is therefore at once a desideratum and a fact. Potentially it is a 'wonderful force' in human life, but it requires unremitting devotion to bring out all its latent quality. The return to the homeland is in Kook's view a national revival which will bring about eventually a religious renaissance, for only in the Land of Israel can the Jewish people live a full and integrated religious life. The contemporary return is accordingly the beginning of the process of *ge'ula*. This process begins with the political independence of the State of Israel and the physical restoration and reclamation of the land. The physical revival is an essential component of the spiritual redemption. For physical concerns and spiritual aspirations are inseparable. The sacred cannot exist without the profane. 'The sacred *(kodesh)* and the profane *(chol)* together influence the human spirit and man is enriched by absorbing from each whatever is suitable.' Indeed, the sacred can exist only so long as it rests upon 'a foundation of the profane', since spiritual sanctity must rest upon the solid base of normal life. No man can be holy if he is unaware of the functions of the physical world and takes no close interest in them. The opposite view that holiness is a state of pure spirituality is criticized by Kook for its one-sidedness and lack of balance. Such holiness became prevalent amongst the Jewish people in the course of its long dispersion, when it was cut off from normal existence in its national homeland. In Kook's idiom this is 'the holiness of exile' in contradistinction to 'the holiness of the Land' which is the earthbound, normal type of holiness. The conditions of exile have caused an imbalance in the spiritual life of Jewry, because — lacking normalcy — the Jews necessarily idealized a type of holiness meant to combat and subdue all natural impulses. But the renewal of Jewish life in the Land of Israel will pave the way for a normalization of holiness.

Ben-Gurion's point of departure is not theological. But he, too, sees in the return to the Land of Israel a movement for the radical transformation and regeneration of Jewish life, and he rejects the notion of a purely cultural or spiritual revival. For Zionism is to him utterly meaningless unless it embraces all aspects of life. The inner spiritual meaning of Zionism is its forceful drive to implement in the here-and-now the messianic vision of the redemption. What is spiritual is the motivation, but the redemption *per se* must be complete, embracing matter and spirit.

For both Kook and Ben-Gurion the State of Israel is the beginning of national redemption and it carries the sparks of the universal redemption. The messianic vision of redemption includes not only the deliverance from oppression but the inauguration of an era of social justice, brotherhood and peace among individuals and nations. Since the Zionist movement and the re-establishment of the State of Israel are viewed by David Ben-Gurion as the manifestations of the growing *ge'ula*, he insists on the need for moral content and spiritual meaning of the political redemption. The man who moulded the armed forces of Israel and led them to victory against overwhelming odds has repeatedly asserted that the root of these military victories is the moral and spiritual qualities of the Jewish nation. 'Not by might, nor by power, but by My spirit, saith the Lord of hosts' (Zechariah 4 : 6). What is decisive is the spiritual strength and the moral stamina of the people.

The faith in *ge'ula* has no meaning unless it is intertwined with the firm belief that only through justice and loving kindness can man walk in the way of God (Micah 6 : 8). The essence of the redemptive process, emphasizes Ben-Gurion, is that life in the independent Jewish State should be moulded by truth and kindness, equality and peace. The political freedom of the Jewish people is the first step towards the fulfilment of the universal vision. Ben-Gurion quotes Isaiah 42 : 6 that Israel's task is to be 'a light to the nations'. He interprets this 'light' by referring to the concluding verse : 'To open eyes that are blind, to bring captives out of prison, out of the dungeons where they lie in darkness.' Quoting Isaiah 49, he amplifies that Israel is entrusted with the task to be a light to the nations so that it shall bring salvation to the whole of mankind — and this is the thrust of the redemptive process which has begun with the Jewish people's liberation through the State of Israel.

Over against Ben-Gurion's humanistic exegesis, Rabbi Kook's view of *ge'ula* is wholly theological. His view of the contents and aims of the redemptive process is rooted in the basic premise that there is a profound, intrinsic and abiding interrelationship between religion and ethics. The following passage (translated from the third volume of

Rabbi Kook's *Orot Hakodesh*) illustrates the connection between religious piety and morality.

> Piety is not a value in itself and it should not be counted among man's abilities and virtues. Left to itself piety may pull down man and mankind to the abyss, and it may equally raise them as high as heavens. But just because it has no value in itself, it is capable of receiving all the lights and of containing all the abilities. Each human faculty comes into its own, and then remains invulnerable, only through its relation to piety — which contains all.
> The ideal piety is therefore achieved not so much by preoccupation with itself as by filling it with knowledge and ability, with Tora and religious deeds, with every virtue, with every manifestation of strength and courage, glory and splendour. (...)
> Piety is the most profound kind of wisdom, when it is based on the innermost view of the world. It provides a solid basis for all science and for all Tora study, whether it concerns the holy or the profane.
> When the profane looks for a solid basis it is bound to realize that without piety science merely hovers over the surface of concepts, and that without piety science is not really wisdom. (...)
> Piety should on no account push aside the natural sense of morality, for it would then no longer remain pure piety. The criterion of pure piety is that the natural morality, which is inherent in man's nature, steadily improves as a result of a person's piety, over and above what it would have been without his piety.
> But if there were a kind of piety without whose influence life would have been better both for individuals and the community, and owing to whose influence the power for doing good were weakened — that would be the wrong kind of piety.

Rabbi Kook utterly rejects the idea that there can be a dichotomy between the divine and the morally good. His theological position expresses in a radical manner what is really a Jewish traditional position. Whilst deploring social ideologies that limit their interest to material conditions, Kook severely criticizes 'any ideology that ignores the need of improving the state of the world and the political order, hovering instead in a rarefied spiritual atmosphere and boasting of the perfection of the soul.' A man is religiously righteous only if he acts out all of human life in holiness and strives for the improvement of the human condition. He interprets the vision of *ge'ula* in terms of the biblical Jubilee year (Leviticus 25) as a suspension of all acquisitive economic dealing: 'A year of quiet and peace, without oppressor or master, a year of equality and tranquility, without any particular private property or any special privilege, when divine peace descends upon all mankind. There is no desecration during this year, because there is no rigorous insistence upon the rights of private property.' This is, of course, a utopian vision, but it reflects Rabbi Kook's concern about the acquisitive character of society. Human aspirations should not be locked exclusively in social and economic activities. But the religious ideal imposes an obligation to strive for an ideal society.

This ideal society is identified with the *ge'ula* of an independent Jewish state in the Land of Israel. But Judaism is universalistic in its vision of the ultimate future of humanity. The messianic expectations are expressed in Zechariah's vision (14:9): 'The Lord shall be King over all the earth; in that day shall the Lord be One and His name one.' The aim of *malkhut shamayim*, the kingdom of heaven, is the theme of *alenu*, the concluding prayer of the daily morning service and the opening prayer of the services on the New Year and the Day of Atonement. Elaborating on the meaning of Jewish nationality, Rabbi Kook states: 'Mankind should unite as one family and then all strife and vice that are born of the division of the peoples will disappear.' But it would be disastrous to mistake the hoped-for vision for the present reality. 'Man cannot fly off to Paradise simply by uttering his faith.' Much educational work must be done before men are able to reach out to the universalistic future. This work should be done through national units, each striving towards the future and the final goal. The idea of national redemption is part of the divine scheme of history. The redemptive process of *ge'ula* will fulfil its purpose when it will pave the way for *malkhut shamayim*, the kingdom of God on earth.

WHAT DOES SALVATION MEAN
TO CHRISTIANS TODAY?

DAVID JENKINS [1]

To be human is the gift of God. If we reflect on what this sentence can mean about the origin of being human, the process of being human and the end of being human, then we shall find in it a pointer to what Christians mean by salvation today. Among themselves Christians seem to mean many different things by 'salvation', or to be unclear what they do or should mean, or to give a meaning to salvation which other Christians say should not or cannot be given. None the less I believe that the claim, the faith, the hope implied in the statement that to be human is the gift of God can be shown to unite all Christians. In one way or another this is what Jesus Christ enables us to believe and offers us the chance to practise — that being human has a source, a potentiality and a fulfilment which is given by God, offered by God and secured by God. Therefore being human is not solely at the mercy of time, circumstances and death. We can be saved and fulfilled.

Further, this understanding of being human as the gift of God refers not only to what Christians *do* mean by salvation today. It is also in accordance with what Christians *ought* to mean by salvation today. This is so because it can be shown that the Bible in its main themes, and in the major stories and pictures which give shape to its message, not only supports but actually puts forward this understanding of the gift of God to men so that they might be all that they might be. The main traditional understandings developed in the Christian churches also likewise reflect, in differing ways and despite their distortions in practice, this conviction that man depends upon God for being man and that therefore he can have the highest possible hopes of his humanity. This biblical and this traditional understanding has both its focus and its climax in Jesus who is believed to be the reality of God existing as the reality of man and the reality of that which is human united to the reality of God.

I shall attempt to outline something of what is implied in this understanding of the gift of God to men and especially to see how this relates salvation to the life of men in *history* and the life of men in *community*.

---

[1] Canon DAVID JENKINS, Church of England, is the Director of Humanum Studies of the World Council of Churches.

But first, it is necessary to consider further the connection referred to above between what Christians do mean by salvation and what they ought to mean, a connection effected through the Bible and Christian tradition.

The Christian knowledge that to be human is the gift of God is, in the Christian understanding, itself a gift. That men have this high calling and these divine potentialities is not a deduction but a revelation. (What we *do* mean by salvation must always be related to what we have been shown we ought to mean.) That is to say that the Christian does not *deduce* the basic answer to the question 'What is man ?' nor to the question 'What is salvation ?' These answers are *given* to him. As I shall attempt to show, this giving, for its fulfilment, lies not only in the past but also in the present and in the future. The first and fundamental point lies, however, in the giving, discovered in history, renewed in history and to be fulfilled beyond history. This giving is believed to be God at work or, better still, in this giving God is known. We may even say that to know the giving is to know God.

Now, I do not know how this can best be expressed in other languages. But I would like to try and explain a little further. For my hope is that this contribution towards the discussion of salvation today will be read by many whose mother tongue is not English and so absorbed into a far richer discussion than is possible in one language. For I believe that the glory of God (which is the measureless measure of the fullness and, therefore, of the salvation of man) will shine more brightly for us as we help one another to go beyond the limitations of our mother-tongues by sharing their respective and differing riches. Thus, I do not write 'to know the *gift* is to know God' ; I write 'to know the *giving* is to know God'. I do not want a pure object or thing word which refers to the result of an activity or the detachable effect of an action. I require a word which expresses action itself, which conveys the notion of the presence of energy and which cannot be separated from whoever or whatever is acting, is energizing, is present. This choice of words is called for because God is not deduced from His gifts. He is known in His giving. (As I shall try to show below this is of fundamental importance with regard to the Christian understanding of, and sharing in, the present struggles to be human, that is, to achieve freedom from oppression, from physical degradation and from being overwhelmed in an environment seemingly out of control.)

It must clearly be left for further discussion how far and in what way the idea that I am expressing in the form 'God is known in His giving' could be expressed in Malayalam or Chinese or in an African idiom, let alone in French, German and Spanish or in Russian and Greek.

It is necessary, however, to record a sensitivity to the partiality and limitations of language in a discussion of the meaning of salvation for Christians. For while the meanings are ours (we have to do the speaking, seek the understanding and take responsibility for proclamation and sharing) the salvation is of God. This is the basis behind all meanings which alone gives them power, so it is believed. Further, since salvation is indeed *of God*, it is addressed to, and concerned with, all men, past, present and future and absolutely without exception. For God is the ultimate reality who embraces all reality absolutely without exception. Yet the universality of the salvation cannot be matched by a corresponding universality in the meanings apprehended, expressed or commended. For meanings have to be expressed in language which is of a particular time, place and culture and meanings have to be apprehended in the lives of men lived out in a particular time, place and culture.

But this very problem and paradox of the meaning of salvation for Christians points also to the unique reality and power of salvation as Christians believe it to be offered. For Christians believe that salvation is, ultimately, the giving of God Himself to men so that their humanity is infinitely filled and fulfilled. ('To be human is the gift of God.') But the uniquely Christian understanding of this giving of God is that provided by Jesus Christ, himself seen, received and understood against the stories of God's dealings with men reflected in the Old Testament scriptures. Thus there is no contradiction between the universality, infinitude and absoluteness of God and His giving Himself in, through and to historical particularities. Jesus Christ is the decisive evidence offered to the faith of Christians and for the faith of Christians. He confirms to us that the activity of God Himself ensures that particular moments, historical processes and embodied persons are the places where God is met, known, received and responded to. This activity of God is His universal and all-embracing work of bringing about salvation, i.e. union with Him and with all fulfilled things and persons in Him.

For all human beings, who must live here and now and in particular, the ultimate enjoyment of all this fullness of His salvation lies always in the future but it is likewise always in each human here and now that

God's giving of Himself is to be received and known. There is no other human place for receiving the gift of salvation than where we now are. How could there be ? For we have nowhere else to be and to become human than where we now are, whether for us being human is a tragedy, a joy, a nonsense, a bore or a routine. Thus in the Christian understanding of salvation, whatever particular meanings are found or expressed, there is no necessary contradiction between the universality of salvation (the gift of God Himself to enable men to be human) and the limitations of particular meanings and expressions about salvation. Rather there is, potentially, richness. For, firstly, this particularity is the way God gives Himself to men ; it is in this particularity that men live and develop (or are distorted) as men. Secondly, God's commitment to these particularities of history shows that it is in and through history that He is building up the ultimate richness of what it is to be human. However, there can be contradiction and obstacles to growth rather than contributions to richness if Christians absolutize the temporary and partial meanings which they have been led to give to salvation and forget that being saved is basically living from, by and to God and not meaning, or believing, or doing, any particular set of things. Because God has committed Himself to history in the particularities in which men are and become human there always will be particular things to believe, mean and do. But salvation *is* none of these things, for salvation is God giving Himself to men so that they may be human. Thus salvation is always beyond words and meanings. None the less it is sometimes below or behind words and meanings. That is to say words and meanings can be provoked by the saving presence of God and can point towards Him. For how else could Christians ever be in a position to say such things as I have been saying, such as that to be human is the gift of God and that this statement itself points not to a deduction but to a revelation ?

Here we return explicitly to the connection between what Christians do mean and what they ought to mean when speaking of salvation. Christians hold that in this steady work of giving himself to men God has built up in history a people who have come to know Him in this work and to know Him as the One who does this work. The record of this building up of a people who receive the knowledge of God and develop this knowledge in a continued dealing with God is reflected in the writings of the Old Testament. Here a series of patterns and pictures and stories is offered to us. People discover who they are and how their history makes sense and how they are to make sense of their history (what they can be and what they must do) through encounters with Him who offers identity, sense and purpose in the midst of events.

Abraham, Moses and the prophets discover themselves, their God and the role and possibilities of their people together in the demands and offers of events and circumstances. Similarly the people discover themselves, their God and their future together in circumstances such as those that lie behind the story of the Exodus. The continuing thread in history is the people, with their traditions and understandings building up out of their history. But the people themselves (or prophetic and gifted men working in and through the life of the people) discover that the continuing thread is a continuing and faithful reality and activity who is at work among them, through them and for them.

But there can be no question of this creative and saving activity and reality being identified with them or confined to them. He is not at their disposal or under their control. Rather they depend for their identity and their future on Him. As their history develops so they learn that 'He' who is in the midst of them is also over against them in disturbance, overthrow and judgement in order to reshape them and renew them for their future and their fulfilment. Likewise they come to recognize 'Him' as at work quite as much in the history from which they suffer (e.g. Cyrus is 'His anointed' Is. 45 : 1) as in the history to which they contribute.

It is necessary to refer to this continuing and faithful reality and activity as 'He' and as 'God' in order to be able to speak at all. But it is also necessary to remember that who 'He' is and therefore what the word 'God' refers to is not something that we mean or intend but always something that he reveals. The Old Testament never offers a firm grasp on the identity of God (we do not know who He is in Himself, we are not able to know His name) nor is there clear knowledge in advance of precisely what He will do (He is discovered in and by means of troubling and unexpected events in and after their happening). But what the Old Testament does bear witness to is a steadily built up assurance that He always will be, and that He will always act consistently with Himself in His Work of saving and fulfilling His people. There is, therefore, sustained faith in Him and an established expectation of Him.

Christians are constituted by the discovery that it is Jesus who embodies this faithful expectation. Therefore what Christians do mean by salvation must always be related to what Christians ought to mean by salvation in the light of the records of the discovery of the saving God reflected in the Old Testament ; and in the light of the witness to the embodiment of this saving God in Jesus which is contained in the New Testament. There is no valid or powerful meaning which can be given to salvation which is independent of and out of touch with these records. Salvation depends upon God and we are dependent upon God for our saving knowledge of his saving work. It is to the discovery of this work that these records point. But what Christians can and do mean by salvation is not *settled* by these records. The meaning of salvation cannot be finally settled until it is fully and finally enjoyed. That is to say until men are fulfilled in their being human through receiving the fullness of the life of God in unimpeded relations with Him and with one another. We do not know what this will mean, i.e. what it will be like, what sort of experience it will be. Meanwhile, however, we are concerned with meanings and actions in our present particularities, struggles and hopes. Here we have the opportunity of receiving in our turn and for our times the discovery of who we are and how we are to be and become human. This involved discovering how our history makes sense and how we are to act to make sense of our history through encounters with Him who offers identity, sense and purpose in the midst of events. We have our opportunities of learning and practising how being human is the gift of God. These opportunities arise as we seek to be the Church, i.e. the people who acknowledge the saving God, in the midst of the world and in grappling with this world.

Such attempts to be the Church can arise only because God has already established, and does Himself maintain, His Church, i.e. the people whom he has brought to acknowledge him in and through Jesus Christ. The basis, as always, is what God gives and His continued giving. But being the Church involves also engaging in the present as members of a community which discovers its identity, purpose and hope out of this *present* engagement in the light of both a *backward* reference and a *forward* reference. It is in this sense that the Church (whatever the possible multiplicity of its manifestations) is a community essentially related to salvation. There would be no meaning to and no meaning for salvation available in the world and in history unless there were a community (expressed in many communities) constituted by the experience of the saving God as He has revealed Himself in history and embodied Himself in Jesus. This community is also committed to discovering the development and fulfilment of this experience. But much harm has been done by ever describing this community (or any of these communities) as the saving community. Saving is the work of God and God's concern is with men, with the fulfilling of what it is to be human. The Church is where this God is known and known to be the saving God. But the Church is neither the saving community nor the community of the saved. Rather she is the community of those who for the time being know (who at present embody the knowledge of) God the Saving one who is the Father of Jesus Christ. Thus the Church has the task (partly performed by her very existence) of maintaining and kindling the effective and practical knowledge and hope that to be human is for *all* men the gift of God, i.e. that salvation is a reality, a real offer and a real experience. This task will be found (and has been found) to require and to offer a variety of ways of engaging in the present life of men. These ways will be worked out in accordance with what has already been discovered about the giving of God to men in history for the sake of their being human (the backward reference) and in relation to the sure and certain hope that the gift of being human will be fulfilled in history, through history and beyond history (the forward reference).

The meanings which salvation and the hope of salvation have to take will be produced by the interplay within the Church of the pressures of the backward reference, the forward reference and the opportunities for, and obstacles to, being human as they are at present experienced. This means that salvation will be understood and experienced differently in different parts of the world, in different parts of the Church, under different circumstances and at different times. (The point about this multiplicity of understanding and experience which is to be noted for final discussion in this essay is that *all* such understandings and experiences are without exception both real and *insufficient* in relation to God's saving.) I am taking up here the point I made earlier that God gives us the answer to the questions 'What is man?' and 'What is salvation?' and that these questions are answered from the past through the present into the future. The answer is received in the process of God's giving Himself to man for human fulfilment. The form this development answer takes depends on where men are in their struggle for being human. That is why, as I also said earlier, the apprehension that God is known in His giving is of fundamental importance with regard to the Christian understanding of, and sharing in, the present struggles to be human.

For the place where God is known and His offer of salvation received is always some place where men either know that their humanity is threatened, distorted, oppressed or some place where they become aware of the offer of a greater humanity than they yet enjoy. Indeed, the knowledge of salvation is precisely the knowledge that there is energy at work (the power of the love of God) to make these two places one and the same. That is to say we are able to become aware that wherever and whenever our being human is threatened, limited, being forced into nothing there is also power at work to liberate our being human for something greater, more free, more human. What we do not know is the precise state and fulfilment of that 'something'. It does not yet appear what, as fulfilled human beings, we shall be (cf. I John 3 : 2). But we discover the promise of this fulfilment in the hopeful possibilities of the present.

Thus the knowledge that there is this God who saves us and that therefore there are these infinite possibilities in being human can come whenever men discover themselves to be set free in the face of some experienced obstacle to their being human and when they know themselves to be set free in a way which promises them a future which is for them but which is not dependent upon them although they have a part to play in attaining it.

Three areas in which this knowledge, which is at once of God, of salvation and of being human as a gift, can be enjoyed are, for example, those of receiving the sacraments, enjoying Pentecostal experience and taking part in a revolutionary struggle for freedom. In all of these experiences it is possible to know both *in community* and *in the name of Jesus Christ* that one is offered a human identity and purpose which goes beyond present limitations, which is being built up by a power from beyond oneself and one's group and which points to a future, which will embrace more and more human beings in more and more freedom and mutual enjoyment. By the receiving of the sacrament, by the speaking with tongues, by the involvement in the revolutionary activity one knows that one has an identity, meaning and purpose. One knows that it is good to be human and worth striving to be human despite all the present threats and limitations and, indeed, precisely in and through these obstacles, sufferings and deaths. The power and the gift of God is known in the midst of life as it is now and life as it is now is thereby offered as a gift for discovering human identity and community both now and with all its promise for the future.

At present Christians very often divide themselves from one another as they insist on identifying the place where salvation is to be found as either in the sacraments or in the experience of the Spirit or in revolutionary commitment or whatever. They also clearly abuse and deny their own chosen locus of salvation in dehumanizing and therefore ungodly ways. Thus Pentecostalists can (but need not) neglect the needs and effects of society and rest with selfish exclusivism on their experiences, sacramentalists can (but need not) press transcendentalism and the sheer givenness of God's gifts to the point where they are not merely indifferent to but positively support the status quo even where it is manifestly oppressive, revolutionaries can (but need not) make idols out of the revolutionary process and ideals and so wholly identify themselves with, say, Marxist allies that they share the Marxist inability to love their (class) enemies and exclude bourgeois and other non-revolutionary sinners from all hope of the salvation of God.

But these, and so many other, unhappy possibilities, may and should be seen as thrusting us all back upon what Jesus Christ has to show us and give us of God. He shows us that God has done and will do all that is necessary to save men from all the ways in which they deny, distort and mistake their humanness. This includes saving them from the ways in which they pervert the very means of salvation by taking control of them and absolutizing them instead of receiving them as God's gifts to be filled by God with the changing meaning and effects required by the changes of history.

Jesus Christ was fully committed to history and to particularity. He was a man. It is thus quite clear that men do not find their God-given humanness which is their divine salvation by holding back from commitment to history and in history. This is precisely because God does not hold back from a like commitment. Thus the sacraments of the Church are signs of God's full presence where and when He is needed by men. Likewise many a Pentecostal experience is to be received as God's dwelling with men. The fullness is His. It is the partiality which is ours. Similarly, it cannot be Christian to be half-hearted in the commitment to the revolutionary struggle for human freedom from degradation and oppression. God provides for his salvation to be fully present in all the ambiguities and particularities because He provides for Himself to be fully present. But He is not present in a fashion which does violence to present human incompleteness or to remove human responsibility.

Thus the sacraments can be grossly abused, Pentecostal experience can be an illusion and revolution can also be a tyranny. In any case our enjoyment or use of all these things remains incomplete quite apart from the errors we introduce in our responses. No one anywhere will achieve liberation (whatever it might properly be) in time for most of those living today to enjoy it. We are all strictly limited beings who cannot expect to have all our potentialities fulfilled and enjoyed within the scope of any state of earthly affairs that is remotely conceivable in our life time. Thus the salvation which is God's gift of Himself to enable us to be fully human is a salvation which the Christian believes is offered within, through and beyond the limitations of human life in this world. The ways in which Christians see, receive and experience this offer are many and doubtless need to be more various. For who can rightly exhaust what the infinite God will do for, and show to, the men He is developing for their fulfilment in Himself and in one another ?

Salvation therefore is always something to come in what can be described only as God's own time and God's own place. But it will come because it has come. God has identified Himself with man's own times and man's own places by being Jesus Christ. And all this can be known because salvation does come. Men and women are renewed in the whole range of human circumstances from joy and freedom to oppression and death. They are given the courage, the purpose and the hope to receive their lives as a gift with infinite potentialities for themselves in relation to the future of all humanity.

In closing I must revert to the limitations of language. Language is inadequate for expressing the meaning of salvation for Christians in at least two ways. Firstly, we are dealing with the whole process of the giving of God Himself to men so that the humanity of all men and women may be fulfilled. And this is clearly a process beyond any description or any experience yet available to any of us. Secondly, we speak different human languages and can convey to one another only fragments of our as yet fragmentary experience. As a slight recognition of this necessary limitation and lack of fulfilment in our knowing about and speaking of God and of the salvation which is God for us and in us, I suggest two bare verbal skeletons which may serve to point to what Christians have meant, do mean and will mean by salvation.

Firstly,   God is.

He is as He is in Jesus.

Therefore there is hope of being human.

Secondly, Men have needs.

        God is at work to meet these needs,

        In and through Jesus.

The giving of living and saving flesh and blood to these or any other verbal skeletons arises in the life, language and circumstances of men and women in their particular communities as they discover that living and dying are gifts with a future for themselves and for their fellow human beings.

UNITY AND ALIENATION IN ISLAM

Hasan Askari [1]

What is possible within the limits of this brief discourse is to introduce, as a first step, the Islamic concepts of God and man. We shall be referring, as occasion arises, to what is mentioned in *Qur'an* which the Muslims hold as the Revealed Word of God. *Qur'an* is therefore the chief source of knowledge of what Islam is. It is the singular document which defines and shapes the life and the thought of every Muslim. The influence which the *Qur'an* possesses over the Muslim mind, and the esteem in which it is held, have not been affected by the passage of time, nor qualified by the various cultural and racial backgrounds which constitute its adherents. Preserved in letter and word, recited and read more frequently than any other scripture, *Qur'an* is regarded by the Muslims as unsurpassed in its authenticity and validity. It is an enigma for the perplexed, a rock of certitude for the grateful and the believing, a challenge for the thought and a judge for the spirit. As a reminding and a warning it thunders against the forgetfulness of man, and awakens him to the awareness and the presence of the transcendent Absolute.

Before we discuss *what* the Islamic formulations are, let us first clearly designate what *kind* of formulations they are. One might be disposed to treat Islamic metaphysics in the mode of general metaphysics. '*There is no Divinity besides the only Divinity*' is a proposition which could be thoroughly discussed after a purely metaphysical mode. However comprehensive and profound, organized and coherent such a metaphysical discourse might be, it will not be able to grasp another aspect of this proposition : its specific character of being a *testimony* and a *witnessing*. The metaphysical sentence which is merely a proposition is transformed by a religious context into an act of testimony. In other words, the reflective act which a proposition signifies changes into an act of bearing testimony and witness. Herein lies the difference between the philosopher *(hakim)* and the prophet *(nabi)*. The same object, the Absolute, is an object of reflection for the philosopher, but for the prophet it is an object of witness.

'*There is no God but God*' is a reflective act. *I bear witness* that there is no God but God should be an act of testimony. Again, at the stage of

---

[1] Dr Askari is Reader in Sociology, Osmania University, Hyderabad, India.

testimony, the stress is on the reflective proposition. The Absolute is still at an abstract level of cognition. The testimony, in order to be complete, must transform into an act of prayer: '*O My God*'. The Absolute is now a full religious object. The religious process is distinct from the metaphysical process. The former moves towards a progressive form of commitment: *reflection-testimony-prayer*. The latter moves towards a progressive form of abstraction: *prayer-testimony-reflection*. The *first* specific character of the Islamic formulations will rest then on the fact that their reflective constituents which look like propositions are in fact acts of testimony and prayer. This refers to their *form*.

The *second* specific character of the Islamic formulations pertains to their *source*. The Islamic source of knowledge is Revelation *(wahi)*. This is not simply to say that man's reflective reason is inadequate, and is perpetually in need of the Revealed Truth from God. The Islamic view does not discredit human reason so categorically. Human reason is not inherently incapable of comprehending the Absolute. Revelation does not come to a man who possesses a crippled and an incomplete reason. Revelation is not a complement to reason, nor its better part, nor a new mode of knowledge. It is a special form of reminding and recollection. It refers to the condition of man upon the earth where what he calls truth *(haq)* is not truth, but a semblance of truth *(zun)*. But *zun* does not refer to any basic deformity of reason *(aqal)*. *Zun* (possessing of a semblance of truth and believing that it is the truth) is the function of *being in the world*, and the *mode* of this being in the world is *forgetfulness (ghafala)*. Revelation is addressed to the forgetful being of man, to his being in the world. It breaks that muteness which is a part of the forgetful self. The supernatural command *to speak (qul)* is a bursting forth of a memory, a recollection of a long-forgotten covenant *(misaq)*. '*There is no God but God*' will now mean '*Do you still remember* that there is no God but God?' Hence, in Islam, there is no such thing, in principle, as conversion, but restoration, a returning and a remembering. *Zikr*, a word that usually stands for prayer, basically means remembering, recollecting, repeating. When a believer says that there is no God but God, he is in fact saying that he *remembers* that there is only One God. *The greatest challenge upon this earth is not so much to explore a God as to remember that there is One.*

The *third* specific formulation refers to the question of *identity*. As revelation is an event when God awakens man from his forgetfulness, it should *happen* to a person, for a people, at a place. A sentence like the following dramatizes the entire principle : God spoke to Moses at Sinai and commanded him to go to Egypt. It is in the very character of a revelation that it involves a prophet, a people and a land. As a reminding, the revelation makes the prophet the first who is awakened from sleep and forgetfulness. Being the first wakened, he becomes the first witness. Being the first witness, he becomes the object of testimony for his people. Hence, the second testimony of Islam : I bear witness that Mohammed is the Prophet of God. To remember God is to remember the Prophet. One testimony is supported by another. As the testimony of God was not complete unless it was transformed into an act of prayer, similarly the testimony of the Prophet should become an act of obedience. One should now say : '*O My Master !*'

As revelation presupposes that man possessed the knowledge of God, what should the concept of prophethood presuppose ? Obviously, if revelation is an address of reminding, the prophet is an addressee who is reminded. But the question is much more complicated. Here, recollection does not refer to what man has learnt during his finite life and has later forgotten ; it rather refers to the primeval dawn of creation when God held the whole of humanity in covenant and all mankind had then said that He was their Lord.

> And when thy Lord brings forth from Adam's children — out of their loins — their offspring and makes them *witnesses against their own selves* by saying : 'Am I not your Lord ?' they say, 'We bear witness.' This He does lest you should say on the Day of Resurrection, 'We were surely unaware of this.' *Qur'an* 7 : 173.

The prophetic act of recollection is thereby a tremendous act. To recollect here is to contradict the testimony of the senses and of the reflective mind as it perceives and ponders. To bear witness here is to bear witness '*against their own selves*'. The hiddenness of God might be taken lightly by man. When the entire world lures the mind to consider it as final and ultimate, the prophet rises to bear witness against it. It is in him that the two testimonies, one of the finite reason and another of revelation, are brought into harmony. But the medium of this harmony is a high spiritual tension. *Qur'an* mentions the likeness of the prophet to other human beings. This likeness refers to the testimony of the finite reason. He is like any other man *(bashr)* but he is the receiver of revelation *(wahi)* too. There is evidence of the divine testimony within him.

It is the Muslim faith that prophecy ended with Mohammed. He is the Seal of all Prophets. It does not mean that the Muslim is limiting God's freedom to send more prophets in the future, but rather it signifies that in Islam man is clearly and unmistakably warned, his forgetfulness has been fully challenged, and that by making the Islamic revelation final, man is made an argument against himself. No other prophet will ever come to remind him again. He has been clearly reminded. This is not as important as it seems at first sight. The essential nature of man with all his real and potential being does not suffer at the hands of revelation. On the contrary, man's real and potential self is unfolded and enriched by the revelatory message. It is a question of hope that a Prophet might come again and lift man from his sleep. The Islamic faith that no such prophet shall ever come places the Muslim in an extraordinary relationship with the *remaining* time upon the earth. The Day of Judgment is brought very near to him. The end of the world is always in sight. Hence, the Muslim anxiety to preserve the *Qur'an* in history. This light should not extinguish.

This brings us immediately to the *fourth* character of the Islamic formulations : their eschatology. There are five components of the eschatological perspective of Islam. They are :

1. *The world is meaningful*. It is not just a sport without purpose. A serious point is involved in being here. For the keen and the observing, there are 'signs' in nature, in mankind, in the hidden self of man. There is order and number, measure and limit, for everything. A true believer does not show his impatience with the world. He ponders, he waits.

2. *The world has an end*. It has a beginning and an ending. It is not self-supporting. It is ephemeral, and it changes. There are again 'signs' of this for the humble and the patient. Everything, whatever is in it, shall perish, except the Face of God. Each river has to run its full course, and oceans have to wait for their final overturning and emptying. As it was once — nothing and emptiness — so shall it be again. There is nothing to set aside or horde, for everything, the owner and his possessions, shall pass into nothingness.

3. *The world shall rise again*. However, there is no meaning in the world if it is to perish for ever. For what then are the patient and the humble waiting for ? For whom has the world run full course ? When will truth and falsehood, justice and injustice be eternally separated ? Should

their distinction be granted only to a few, the seers and the prophets, or should all mankind know in one glimpse as one resurrected assembly ? Everyone will be called from death and dust. Nothing shall be lost. It will be a day of great disillusionment both for the denying and the self-righteous. They will wish that they had been dead for all eternity. This reconstruction of their being will be a burden and a distress for them. Those who have shunned death shall now yearn for it. It was for this day that both God and those who believed in Him without seeing Him have waited for so long.

4. *The world shall be judged.* Judgment is a full consummation of the idea of meaning. What was ambiguous should now become clear. What was mixed should now part. Justice will then mean the total manifestation of the spontaneous and the natural relation between faith and heaven, between denial *(kufr)* and hell.

5. *The world shall be at peace with God.* The disorder will give way to order. The uncertainty of the believer and the doubt of the unbeliever will then dissolve. The pious and the humble, who have believed in God without quarrelling and reservation, will *agree* with God, and God will *agree* with them. The wound of the earth will be permanently healed. Neither pain nor death, neither life nor its vanity, will screen man from his God. The world, even today, with all its conflict and discord, war and hate, is *disposed* towards that Day, and the *peace* of that Day.

The Muslim's faith is a unity of the revelatory, the prophetic, and the eschatological perspectives. They are all blended in his life and work. Man himself is perhaps a unity of these perspectives. Yet it seems in some respect that Islam is in perpetual battle with history. Let us look again at the Islamic view of man, from a different standpoint.

The *myth* of Adam's creation, as mentioned in *Qur'an*, lends itself to analysis, and we abstract, from it, three ontological states of man. The word 'myth' should not be mistaken for something unreal or fantastic. By myth we mean here a particular form of knowledge and mode of expression.

The *first ontological state* pertains to the condition of Adam before he had approached the forbidden tree. This has three characteristics : *Divinity*, *Knowledge*, and *Power*. *Divinity* refers to the nature of man as made after the Nature of God. 'And follow the Nature of God — the Nature in which he has created mankind.' *(Qur'an 30 : 31)*. As such, man becomes an object of worship by angels. 'And when we said to the angels, "Submit to Adam",... they all submitted.' *(Qur'an 2 : 35)* *Knowledge* refers to the fact that God did not leave Adam in darkness, but allowed him to know who was his Creator and Lord. Adam was equally well instructed concerning the world of creation. 'And He taught Adam all the names.' *(Qur'an 2 : 32) Power* reflects man's sovereignty over the earth and the skies, his dominion over bird and beast, over air and water. 'Thy Lord said to the angels : "I am about to place a vicegerent in the earth".' *(Qur'an 2 : 31)* Man, shaped after the nature of his Lord, bestowed with knowledge, and given dominion over the entire world, was a noble and a glorious creation. It was God's love for Adam that made him receive such rare gifts, that made angels worship him, that made Satan envious.

The *second ontological state* as we follow the myth of Adam concerns what follows when he has eaten the forbidden fruit. There are two stages. *First* is Adam and Eve's consciousness of being naked as soon as they tasted the forbidden fruit. This was the beginning of the departure from their original divinity and closeness to God. Shame had taken the place of love. The principle of difference and duality, that they were man and woman, was the consequence of shame, of deep rupture between God and man. Adam had already fallen from his first ontological state. Awareness of acute distress and fear at having disobeyed the Lord had already taken away Divinity, Knowledge, and Power from Adam. He was in deep agony.

Second, God responds to Adam's distress in an act of overflowing love, and teaches him the words of repentance. 'Then Adam learnt from his Lord certain words of prayer. So he turned towards him with mercy. He is oft-returning with Compassion, and is Merciful.' *(Qur'an 2 : 38)* Adam was thus cared for, and his original sin was forgiven.

The *third ontological state* commences when God asks Adam and Eve to 'go forth' from heaven. 'Go forth ; some of you are enemies of others, and for you there is an abode in the earth and a provision for a time.' *(Qur'an 2 : 37)* The departure that began with the eating of the forbidden fruit is now complete. Man is separated from God, and undergoes a vast change, from love to shame, from joy to fear, from unity to multiplicity, from peace to discord, from abundance to want, from confidence in God to pain and suffering, from nearness to separation and longing. But God's love again overflows. He supports man with hope and promise. 'We said, "Go forth, all of you, from here.

And if there comes to you guidance from Me, then whosoever shall follow my guidance, on them shall come no fear, nor shall they grieve." '
(Qur'an 2 : 39)
Man goes forth into the world not as a damned and cursed being but as one in crisis.

His being in crisis is what he carries within himself : the three vastly different but interwoven states and experiences, *nearness with God, anxiety about God, separation from God.* The three selves of which *Qur'an* speaks, the carnal self *(ammara)*, the self-accusing spirit *(Lovwama)* and the soul at rest *(mutmainna)*, recall again the three ontological states of man. The three spheres, regularly mentioned in *Qur'an* — the heavens *(samawat)*, the earth *(arz)*, and what is in between *(bainu-huma)* — further illustrate the multiplicity of man's being as a source of his crisis.

The most crucial state is the third, man having left heaven and come upon earth, under the dominion of his carnal self. The archetype Adam is confronted with the race of man. Imagine the horror of a person who sees himself countlessly sub-divided into more and more men across the earth down the unending corridor of time. Having been once *one*, and having been once *near* God, this multiplicity and distance must be an awful experience.

Man's being in crisis consists in having been once near God, one with God. The supreme moment of religion is the lowest moment in man's being, namely, separation from God. It is in the pain and the cloud of this suffering that man becomes conscious of his spiritual origin, and of the vast distance that separates him now. The noble and the divine in him is torn away. The repenting and the yearning spirit wanders to reach its destiny, and falters on the way.

Even if man succeeds in reconstructing the unity of his spirit, he will still be in perpetual fear of God, which is not as God made him. Man has then to wait on God, for the hand of God alone shall remake him. The entire eschatological perspective of Islam lies in this act of waiting. As man waits, so also God waits. To wait, for man, is to be patient, not to hurry, not to press the divine plan, not to demand miracles, not to insist on the end of the world, not to cross the limits. What is faith ? 'Verily we are from God and unto God we return.' It is the awareness of the irresistible movement of one's self back to its source. Verily we are from God *and* unto God we return. The origin and the end are clear and certain. But in that '*and*' lies the vast mystery and the yearning, the weight of movement through life upon the earth. The conjunction is the symbol of delay, of waiting, of anxiety, of labour, of alienation. But it is also the link and the convergence of the divine origin and end in man. It is by heightening the tension of alienation that the condition of unity can be apprehended. Adam's distress at having disobeyed his Lord was also the occasion of suffering at his separation from Him. As God forgave him, he was assured that He was not far. There must be a subtle belonging between 'going forth' and 'returning'.

The world, unlike man, is a direct expression of the will of God. The entire universe is disposed towards God, prostrates before Him, and is engaged in an unending praise of His Lordship and Glory. They are 'muslim' in the sense that they have fully surrendered to God. They have no option. There is no difference between their being and their submission. But man is different. He has the *choice* to deny and revolt against God or to praise and submit to Him. Was choice a part of the original being of man? What is implied in 'choosing'? Obviously, freedom. Did God make man free? We believe that God bestowed upon Adam freedom as well as Nobility, Knowledge and Power. When the angels objected to Adam's creation and said that he would spread discord and shed blood, God had replied that He knew what they knew not. What could be outside the orbit of the knowledge of the angels? They knew their God, His whole creation, what was and what should come about. Their objection that Adam would spread discord in the earth proved that they possessed the knowledge of the future too. The greatest probability is that they knew all but one intention of God, the intention to make man free. Freedom was foreign to the being of the angels. They were shaped, like the whole world, after the will of God, to bow before its authority, to surrender without question. Because the angels had objected at the very first moment of Adam's creation and God had admonished them that He knew what they knew not, it becomes clear that freedom was not a consequence of disobedience or guilt but an original condition of man's being. God had created man noble, knowing, sovereign and free. In nobility, knowledge and sovereignty, Adam was like all the rest of creation. It was only in the capacity to be free that he had no equal. Hence, God's command to angels : 'Prostrate before Adam.'

Disobedience was not the birth of freedom but a violation of the freedom man already had. Going forth from heaven was not the beginning of freedom but the price of possessing it. When God said, 'Go forth and have your habitation in the earth, and have provision for a time', He had qualified the ontological freedom (freedom proper to the being of man) into a temporal freedom (freedom with the awareness of its end). *Hence, the myth of the creation of Adam was also a myth of the creation of time.* This 'time' was a lacune, a chasm, a gap, an abnormality in the order of creation. It is a veil that God draws upon His face, an opportunity for those who know and believe, a forgetfulness that comes upon the blind and the unknowing, a discordant note in the music of the universe.

Freedom and *time* are overwhelming for man. He is awed and mystified by them. He is himself a *mysterium tremendum* now, wishing to accord himself a divinity and a lordship which his freedom and his provision upon the earth would fairly justify. But there is a counterproposition: There is no Divinity besides the One Divinity. The myth of Adam's creation, repeated in *Qur'an* on several occasions, is a reminder that man's freedom and his time are judge and evidence against him. Each trait by which God draws man to Himself — nobility, knowledge, power, and freedom — is at the same time an occasion of man's falling away from God. Again, the terms of unity are also the terms of alienation.

So far, we have been considering the nature and the expression of alienation and estrangement of man *from God*. Is God also estranged *from man*? It seems that, in the Christian tradition, God, having condemned man to his earthly state, envious that he might 'put forth his hand and take also of the tree of life, and eat, and live for ever', is estranged from man. But God, in *Qur'an*, is not affected by what Adam has done to himself. God is generous to man on all occasions: He loves all the Adams: the Adam of His likeness, the Adam who committed the sin, the Adam who asked for repentance and mercy, the Adam who was forgiven, the Adam who was granted freedom and 'provision for a time', the Adam who was promised revelation and divine guidance. The concept of God's love in *Qur'an* seems to be incomparably vaster than that of the Old Testament. *Man is alienated from God, but God is not alienated from man.* 'The Divine Being is not veiled from us, we are veiled from Him and it is for us to try to rend this veil asunder, to try to know God.'[2]

---

[2] NASR, S. H.: *Ideals and Realities in Islam.* London: Allen and Unwin, p. 21.

God is *near*. Only man is far from Him. Man's estrangement does not cause resentment in God. He is compassionate and understanding. Lest man despair of His Lofty Being, of His Absoluteness and Distantness, He makes his prophet say to his companion : 'Grieve not, for God is with us.' *(Qur'an 9 : 40)* It is in the nature of the belief in the Transcendent Absolute that it should cause grief *(huzn)*. God's Being as Far, as Above, must cause sadness. The sense of *nearness* of God, of the Almighty Lord, is equally disconcerting. Such proximity with the Absolute should naturally bring about immense *fear*. Again God says, *fear not (la-taqaf)*. Both Grief and Fear are the conditions of faith in the Absolute who is both *far* and *near*. A believer might get lost either in grief, in the awareness of the inaccessible Absolute, or in fear, in the sense of the nearness of the Absolute. It is only in the proper appreciation of grief and fear and their surpassing that a believer finds rest. Then, God becomes *Peace*. It is in this name of God that His Absolute Transcendence and His Nearness are harmonized. There is an extraordinary affinity between these two Arabic words, *iman* (faith) and *aman* (peace). The root of *islam* is *salam*, *salama*, again meaning peace or to be at peace. The principle of the unity of God in Islam is a principle of peace which God is. The alienation of man is his struggle to transcend *grief* and *fear*, to know God beyond *transcendence* and *nearness*, to know as both Transcendent and Near. God, as *Peace*, is above all estrangement.

To utter the word God is to regather all the threads of the universe, and to return to its centre, the hidden peace and stability behind all discord and change. To believe in God is to reaffirm freedom from the finality of the world, and to reaffirm freedom is to again mistrust the medium of our existence, namely, *time*. This is the last fetish, but an essential fetish, for all civilization rests on the *trust of time*. As philosophy rests on the trust of words, so civilization rests on the foothold of time, and, as such, it resists the idea of *end of time*. Yet with each successive stage in the triumph of the idea of time as a trustworthy medium, there is a corresponding decrease in freedom. What was once a cause for envy in the whole of creation, is given up with ease and indifference. Moreover, the contradiction in the very medium of time is not noticed. The modern city is the embodiment and artifice of pseudo-eternity. People within the city run on and on *panting* for time. It is like running a long race — the track is of course long, stable and continuous (just like time which is there, and will continue endlessly) but the runner constantly gasps for breath.

Alienation is exactly this breathlessness, panting and gasping for time, while freedom is the ability to run fast. The very thing man has supposedly conquered, recoils against him.

To utter the word God is to raze the edifice of pseudo-eternity to the ground, to declare again that man is free.

A MARXIST VIEW OF LIBERATION

AJIT ROY [1]

The Marxist view of liberation is not concerned with the individual quest for salvation in isolation from the social milieu. It is a perspective of man's fulfilment within the general stream of socio-historical evolution. According to Marxism, human bondage since the dawn of civilization has been the product of the mutual inter-action (dialectic, to use the exact Marxist term) between a particular human society as a whole and its natural environment, and between social groups, i.e. classes, of human beings. Man can achieve his liberation only by changing these relationships.

In the far-off pre-historic period, when man knew neither how to control fire nor how to make tools, human groups wandering from forest to forest and cave to cave were totally dominated by natural forces. Through millenia of collective practice, man gradually learnt to control fire and to produce simple tools. Thus began the historical voyage of liberation from the bondage of nature. In this process, however, conditions were created for a new bondage — man's subjugation by man through the division of the community into two classes; one class exploiting and oppressing the other.

It was this division of society into classes that created conditions for an accelerated development of knowledge, science and technology during the long course of social evolution and has now brought human society to a stage where the *potential* has been created for 'securing for every member of society... an existence not only fully sufficient materially, and becoming day by day more full, but an existence guaranteeing to all the free development and exercise of their mental and physical faculties'.[2] This potential, however, can only be realized by carrying through a revolutionary reorganization of society, i.e. by the abolition of classes and the socialization of production. The need for revolution is increased by two further results of the same course of development : i. the degradation of man under class domination and ii. the accumulation of crisis forces in the present social system, entailing colossal wastage of social resources and tremendous retardation in the growth of productive forces.

---

[1] Mr ROY is editor of *The Marxist Review*, Calcutta, India.
[2] ENGELS, F. : *Anti-Dühring*. Moscow : Progress Publishers, p. 335.

Under the present capitalist system vast masses of people, deprived of the ownership of the means of production, must sell their labour power in order to live, to capitalists who have concentrated ownership in their hands. But does this sale of their labour power enable the proletarian masses to really live as men ? Marx answered this question in this way :

> The exercise of labour power, labour, is the worker's own life-activity, the manifestation of his own life. And this *life-activity* he sells to another person in order to secure the necessary *means of subsistence.* Thus his life-activity is for him only a means to enable him to exist. He works in order to live. He does not even reckon labour as part of his life. It is a commodity which he has made over to another. Hence, also, the product of his activity is not the object of his activity. What he produces for himself is not the silk he weaves, nor the gold he draws from the mines, nor the palace he builds. What he produces for himself is *wages,* and silk, gold, palace resolve themselves for him into a definite quantity of the means of subsistence, perhaps into a cotton jacket, some copper coins and a lodging in a cellar. And the worker, who for twelve hours weaves, spins, drills, turns, builds, shovels, breaks stones, carries loads, etc., does he consider this twelve hours' weaving, spinning, drilling, turning, building, shovelling, stone breaking as a manifestation of his life, as life ? On the contrary, life begins for him where his activity ceases, at table, in the public house, in bed. The twelve hours' labour on the other hand has no meaning for him as weaving, spinning, drilling, etc., but as *earnings* which bring him to the table, to the public house, into bed.[3]

The real implications of the situation thus created were brought out by Marx in an earlier writing of his :

> Man (the worker) no longer feels himself to be really active in any but his animal functions — eating, drinking, procreating, or at most in his dwelling and in dressing-up, etc. ; and in his human functions he no longer feels himself to be anything but an animal. What is animal becomes human and what is human becomes animal.[4]

There is no more glaring example of how workers become the ever cheaper commodity, the more they produce, than in the USA, whose dazzling glitter and affluence are mostly cited as the best defence of the *status quo.* The persistence of a large area of misery in the United States finds recognition in the much-publicized, but little waged, official 'war on poverty'.

---

[3] MARX and ENGELS : *Selected Works*, Vol. 1. Moscow, 1950, p. 77.
[4] MARX, KARL : *Economic and Philosophical Manuscripts of 1844.* Moscow, p. 73.

According to official US definitions, family units with incomes below $3,000 a year and unattached individuals with an annual income of less than $1,500 should be regarded as poor. By this reckoning about 20 per cent of US citizens live below the poverty line. But there are unofficial estimates which put the figure of the poor and 'deprived' segment of the American population at a much higher level, sometimes estimated to be as high as one third of the nation. The proportion of the population below the poverty line is much higher among blacks and other underprivileged groups such as the Puerto Ricans.[5]

Side by side with this colossal poverty in the richest country in the world is the equally colossal wastage of social resources on arms and war. According to one estimate, between 1948 and 1965 (inclusive) the United States spent a total of $734.2 billion on defence. Commenting on this huge military expenditure, an American economist posed the question : 'What happens, however, if this trend of defence expenditure takes the opposite direction ? Suppose through some miraculous advance in civilization, the world disarms and lives in peace ?' He replied : 'If disarmament were total and precipitate, hardly anyone could doubt that America's economy would sink into chaos, dependent as it is today on ever-increasing defence expenditure. Total disarmament is doubtless a dream, though America did disarm completely only a generation ago. But even a partial disarmament would pose difficult, if not insurmountable, economic readjustment.'[6]

This coexistence of mass poverty and wasteful or destructive expenditure is not a coincidence. It is the inescapable result of the contradiction between the high productivity of socialized labour and the narrow limits of effective demand ordained by the private appropriation of the fruits of labour. It is only through the operation of the safety valves of armament and defence expenditure, allocation for space research (which creates an artificial market for a considerable proportion of society's production), and so on, that the present economic system can cushion the shocks of the periodic crises.

The irrational and inhuman nature of the capitalist system — historically the last and highest form of the class society — on the one hand condemns vast masses of the population to an animal existence and, on

---

[5] On April 22, 1968, the Citizens' Board of Inquiry into Hunger and Malnutrition in the United States presented a 100-page report, *Hunger, USA*, to Congress. The report found that more than 10 million were literally starving in the USA, with the most widespread hunger in the South.

[6] KUST, MATHEW J. : 'America's War Economy', in *Economic Times*. Bombay, April 4, 1966.

the other, seeks to channel huge resources into destructive and totally wasteful purposes. It is fully ripe for overthrow. And it has produced its own grave-diggers. When the system has been overthrown and the means of production have been socialized, anarchy in social production is replaced by planned and conscious organization. The struggle for individual existence disappears. For the first time, man, in a certain sense, is finally marked off from the rest of the animal kingdom and emerges from animal to really human conditions of existence. The whole of life which conditions man, and which hitherto has ruled man, now comes under the dominion and control of man. For the first time he becomes the real and conscious lord of nature because he has become master of his own social organization. The laws of social action, which previously have been presented as the law of nature and have dominated and oppressed man, will be used with full understanding, and so mastered by him. Man's own social organization, hitherto confronting him as a necessity imposed by nature and history, now becomes the result of his own free action. Extraneous objective forces that have hitherto governed history pass under the control of man himself. From that time on, man will himself make his own history with full consciousness. Only then will social causes set in movement by him begin to have, in constantly growing measure, the result which he intended. 'It is the ascent of man from the kingdom of necessity to the kingdom of freedom.'[7]

II

The Marxist view of liberation presented above in its barest outline is sometimes misunderstood and misrepresented as a naturalist conception of history which reduces man to a passive factor. Nothing is further from the truth. The passage sings the glory of man — increasingly achieving and asserting his freedom. Engels in his lifetime directly refuted the misrepresentation. He said :

> According to the materialist conception of history, the determining element in history is *ultimately* the production and reproduction in real life. More than this neither Marx nor I have ever asserted. If therefore somebody twists this into the statement that the economic element is the *only* determining one, he transforms it into a meaningless, abstract and absurd phrase. The economic situation is the basis, but the various elements of the superstructure — political forms of the class struggle

[7] ENGELS : *Anti-Dühring*, pp. 335-336.

and its consequences, constitutions established by the victorious class after a successful battle, etc. — forms of law and then even reflexes of all these actual struggles in the brains of the combatants : political, legal, philosophical theories, religious ideas, and their further development into systems of dogma — also exercise their influence upon the course of the historical struggles and in many cases preponderate in determining their *form*...[8]

On another occasion, Engels says :

With man we enter *history*. Animals also have a history, that of their derivation and gradual evolution to their present state. This history, however, is made for them, and in so far as they themselves take part in it, this occurs without their knowledge or desire. On the other hand, the more that human beings become removed from animals in the narrower sense of the word, the more they make their history themselves, consciously, the less becomes the influence of unforeseen effects and uncontrolled forces on this history, and the more accurately does the historical result correspond to the aim laid down in advance. If, however, we apply this measure to human history, to that of even the most developed peoples of the present day, we find that there still exists here a colossal discrepancy between the proposed aims and the results arrived at, that unforeseen effects predominate, and that the uncontrolled forces are far more powerful than those set into motion according to plan. And this cannot be otherwise as long as the most essential historical activity of men, the one which has raised them from bestiality to humanity and which forms the material foundation of all their other activities, namely, the production of the means of subsistence, that is, today, social production, is particularly subject to the interplay of unintended effects of uncontrolled forces and achieves its desired aim only by way of exception and, much more frequently, the exact opposite.[9]

Marx concludes his *Theses on Feuerbach* with the following epigram which is the quintessence of the Marxist world outlook : 'The philosophers have only *interpreted* the world, in various ways : the point, however, is to change it.' [10]

III

The liberation of the peoples of the vast Asian continent has always featured prominently in Marxian thought for two fundamental reasons. First, as exponents of the deepest humanism, Marxists, especially Marx

---

[8] MARX and ENGELS : *Letters*. Calcutta, 1945, pp. 417-18.
[9] MARX and ENGELS : *Selected Works*, Vol. II, p. 69.
[10] MARX, KARL : *Theses on Feuerbach*, p. 367.

himself, were appalled by the extreme degradation of men in the utterly stagnant societies of India and China. Second, with the extension of the colonial empires of the European capitalist powers on the Asian continent, the colonies became the source and reservoir for the economic and military strength of the metropolitan powers. Hence the struggle for the liberation of the European proletariat came to be organically linked with the struggle for the liberation of the peoples of Asia.

Marx mercilessly exposed the misery to which men were condemned in traditional Indian society :

> These idyllic village communities, inoffensive though they may appear, had always been the solid foundation of Oriental despotism, in that they restrained the human mind within the smallest possible compass, making it the unresisting tool of superstition, enslaving it beneath traditional rules, depriving it of all grandeur and historical energies. We must not forget the barbarian egotism which, concentrating on some miserable patch of land, had quietly witnessed the ruin of empires, the perpetration of unspeakable cruelties, the massacre of the population of large towns, with no other consideration bestowed upon them than on natural events, itself the helpless prey of any aggressor who deigned to notice it. We must not forget that this undignified, stagnatory and vegetative life, that this passive sort of existence evoked on the other part, in contradistinction, wild, aimless, unbounded forces of destruction, and rendered murder itself a religious rite in Hindustan. We must not forget that these little communities were contaminated by distinctions of caste and by slavery, that they subjugated man to external circumstances instead of elevating man to be the sovereign of circumstances, that they transformed a self-developing social state into never changing natural destiny, and thus brought about a brutalizing worship of nature, exhibiting its degradation in the fact that man, the sovereign of nature, fell down on his knees in adoration of *Hanuman*, the monkey, and *Sabbala*, the cow.[11]

He was equally scathing about China.

The question of the further evolution of society in both India and China was viewed by the founders of the Marxist science as part of the question of world revolution. 'The question is', said Marx, 'can mankind fulfil its destiny without a fundamental revolution in the social state of Asia ?' [12]

---

[11] MARX, KARL: 'British Rule in India', in MARX and ENGELS: *On Colonialism*. Moscow, pp. 36-7.
[12] *Ibid.*, p. 37.

IV

In the Marxist view, the liberation of the Asian people involves struggle in three successive stages; first, freedom from colonial or neocolonial domination; second, the abolition of classes, and, finally, liberation from the thraldom of nature. However, these essentially distinct stages partly overlap inasmuch as the colonial or neocolonial domination over a country is exercised with the collaboration of some of the indigenous classes or strata. Without striking at them, the colonial or neocolonial regime cannot be eliminated. Similarly, it is only by partly freeing the masses, or at least their revolutionary vanguard, from the bondage of nature by ridding them of their fatalistic and subservient attitude towards the existing order and imbuing them with the scientific world outlook, that the struggle for liberation can be carried forward.

In these battles, the Marxists in Asia had, and still have, to challenge the reformist and/or revivalist trends which, often couched in the traditional idiom of the masses, find a ready response among the relatively backward sections of the Asian peoples. Gandhism is an eminent example of the sort of approach the Marxist had, and still has, to contend with. It should, however, be stated in parentheses that Gandhism as an ideology was not exactly synonymous with the tactics and methods of mass struggles against the British domination in India led by Gandhi. The mass movements led by Gandhi made an invaluable contribution to the evolution of Indian history by unleashing vast popular forces in the political arena for the first time and breaking down the legal-constitutional framework that constricted the liberation struggle before his advent on the Indian political scene. But his ideological orientation always remained backward-looking, as may be seen from the excerpts from his writings quoted below. In 1908, Gandhi wrote in *Hind Swaraj* :

We have managed with the same kind of plough as existed thousands of years ago. We have retained the same kind of cottages that we had in former times, and our indigenous education remains the same as before. We have had no system of life-corroding competition. Each followed his own occupation or trade, and charged a regulation wage. It is not that we did not know how to invent machinery, but our forefathers knew that, if we set our hearts after such things, we would become slaves and lose our moral fibre. They, therefore, after due deliberation decided that we should only do what we could with our hands and feet. They saw that our real happiness and health consisted in a proper use of our hands and feet. They further reasoned that large cities were a spare and a useless encumbrance and that people would not be happy in them, that there would be gangs of thieves and robbers, prostitution and vice in them, and that poor men would be robbed by rich men. They were, therefore, satisfied with small villages.[13]

It will be seen from the above that what Marxism deplores in the stagnatory and vegetative life of the atomized villages in pre-British days was admired and cherished by Gandhi. He wanted to take the nation as near to those conditions as possible. Leaving aside the question of the desirability of such a choice, it is just not feasible — the wheels of history cannot be put into reverse. That is why even those who put Gandhi on a pedestal as the Father of the nation were not guided by his ideals in shaping the basic state policies of independent India. Nehru, Gandhi's devoted disciple and political heir, developed his own model for the post-independence evolution of the country and called it the *socialistic pattern of society*. The model had modernization and large-scale industrialization as its central aims.

But notwithstanding the frequency of socialistic phraseology, Nehru's model did take over the essential principle of Gandhian ideology : the coexistence, as opposed to the abolition, of classes. Chapter 1 of the *Third Five-Year Plan*, reported to be the handiwork of Nehru himself, makes repeated reference to 'socialism', 'socialist patterns of society', and even the 'transition towards socialism'. Needless to say, these terms are not used to connote the scientific concept of socialism, i.e. the abolition of private property in the means of production and the establishment of social ownership and control. In fact, the plan makes it clear that the private sector, including large-scale enterprise, will remain unmolested. The plan emphasizes the complementary nature of the public and the private sectors. 'With the rapid expansion of the economy', says the plan report, 'wider opportunities of growth arise for both the public and the private sectors and in many ways their activities are complementary... In the context of the country's planned development, the private sector has a large area in which to develop and expand.'

The result of these basic policies, initiated by Nehru and carried through during the quarter century of freedom, has been a steady increase in socioeconomic polarization in the country. Even official surveys and analyses reveal the accelerating rate at which the rich are becoming richer and the poor poorer.

---

[13] GANDHI, M. K. : *Towards Non-violent Socialism*. Ahmedabad : Navajivan Publishers, 1962, pp. 3-4.

Gandhi's lifelong struggle, continued by his disciples after his martyrdom, has not yet succeeded in stamping out even the crudest form of caste oppression that defiles the largest community of the Indian people — the Hindus. Not a year passes without the brutal lynchings of the Harijans — a euphemism coined by Gandhi himself to denote the so-called untouchables — who continue to constitute the base of the caste-class pyramid of the Indian society.

The future, therefore, contains the prospect of sharper battles in the socio-political arena. On the one hand, the Indian bourgeoisie, immensely strengthened during the last 22 years of accelerated economic development through successive five-year plans, will increasingly be trying to consolidate and extend its influence and authority. The semi-starved, exploited and increasingly disillusioned masses, on the other hand, will increasingly exercise conscious and not-so-conscious pressure for a radical change in the direction of social evolution. Only a conscious leadership guided by the revolutionary science of Marxism can successfully lead the battle of gigantic social forces to achieve the liberation of the teaming millions of the Indian people.

V

Since the Bolshevik revolution in Russia and more particularly since the success of the liberation war in China, socialist and Marxist idioms have become widely popular among the peoples of the Afro-Asian region. Both as a result of this development and as a reaction to it, concepts have emerged such as 'Arab socialism', 'Islamic socialism' and 'African socialism'. Most of these concepts have no fully developed or consistent ideological base. On the whole they may be divided into three broad approaches :

1. An eclectic amalgam of various ideological elements that seeks to express the desire for a freer and juster social order. 'Neither revolution nor socialism', says a critical analyst of recent political developments in the Arab countries, 'had strict theoretical foundations in any of the core countries, but developed pragmatically into various political and economic structures. The emphasis on social justice and economic reform — which the "revolution" sought to realize through "socialism" — was basically moral in character... In some ways, "revolution" and "socialism" really symbolized traditional Islamic social justice.'

2. A revivalist and conservative ideologist trend that seeks to don socialist garb for demagogic purposes. Thus, for instance, the Nigerian sociologist Father Bede Onuoha preaches that the evolution of African socialism 'should be sought in the home-bred socialist pattern bequeathed us by our ancestors' and he proposes 'a return to the wisdom and values of our fathers'. 'The basic principles of African socialism', he says, 'are fraternity, leadership, dialogue, planned development, harmony, autonomy, positive neutrality and pan-humanism. The first three are borrowed from the traditional African concept of family and community, the fourth from world socialism, and the fifth, harmony, is represented as a correction introduced by Africans into the experience of both the economically developed socialist and capitalist countries.' [14]

A critical analysis of this and other similar brands of 'indigenous' socialism reveals the predilections of their sponsors for the basic capitalist framework, with, of course, some modifications.

3. Finally there is discernible in some of these trends in recent years an attempt to adopt and adapt the basic tenets of the Marxist ideology to suit local conditions and meet the demands of the liberation struggle of a largely pre-capitalist country. For instance, the United Arab Republic Charter of National Action says: 'Scientific socialism is the suitable way for arriving at the right method for achieving progress.' Though it warns that Arab revolutionaries cannot afford to copy others, it adds significantly: 'This, however, does not mean that the national struggle of peoples and nations is today required to create new conceptions for its great objectives but rather to find the methods suited to the trend of general evolution and the changing nature of the world.'

It is the duty of Marxists to combat the second trend outlined above while helping the first and the third to ensure that the universal principles of Marxist science may be translated into national practice by the progressive forces of these countries, in accordance with the concrete socio-economic and cultural realities of the respective nation.

VI

Marxism, as Marx and Engels used to stress so persistently, is not a dogma but a guide to action. While pursuing the same ultimate aim, Marxists have to adopt different tactics to suit the varying objective conditions of different countries. It is significant that the first mature document

---

[14] In his *The Elements of African Socialism*. London : A. Deutsch.

of Marxist science, *Manifesto of the Communist Party*, written jointly by Marx and Engels, worked out the main tactical requirements separately for the leading countries of Europe and the USA during the middle of the last century. Hence there can be no stereotype Marxist approach to the tasks of the liberation struggle in Asia. Conditions vary widely from country to country in respect to the degree of pre-capitalist survival, the extent of colonial and neocolonial domination, the development of capitalism, the differentiation among the peasantry and so on. But the common features in Asia and for that matter in all under-developed countries today which distinguish Marxist strategies and tactics, are : i. greater reliance on the revolutionary participation of the peasantry and ii. a greater degree of rapport with the nationalistically inclined bourgeoisie as distinct from the collaborating sections of the bourgeois class.

Among the Marxists themselves, a fierce controversy has been raging for some years about the *modus operandi* of the revolutionary struggle. One section influenced by the Chinese and Cuban experience is inclined towards the adoption of the method of partisan warfare, i.e. the creation of armed guerrilla bands located in relatively inaccessible terrains as the nucleus of a revolutionary army which will gradually expand its operations and finally encircle the urban seats of power and defeat them.

The other trend, oriented towards the policies put forward by the Communist Party of the Soviet Union, is engaged in seeking new advances in cooperation with sections of the progressive bourgeoisie through what is called the non-capitalist path of national democracy. The exponents of this trend believe that this will push through more or less peacefully the transition of the predominantly pre-capitalist society to socialism through industrialization under the aegis of the state and by gradual elimination of the colonial and neo-colonial stranglehold as well as the indigenous exploiting elements.

This controversy, reinforced by the fallout from the now raging Sino-Soviet conflict over wide-ranging issues of theory and practice, has led to a serious loss of cohesion and even to splits in the communist movement in many parts of Asia. This has led to an undoubted loss of credibility in the Marxist path to liberation as a whole. I cannot add much to what I wrote some time ago :

> The questions that admittedly divide the Marxists of the day — the questions of war and peace, of liberation of the subjugated peoples, of new

forms of transition to socialism, of a correct blending of democracy and centralism in a communist party and state, etc., etc., — have come to the fore, not because Marxism has failed in its central task of demolishing the old world and reconstructing a new one. These questions have assumed their present dimensions precisely because Marxism has succeeded in dealing staggering blows to the old world and in creating a mighty edifice of a new one. New horizons have opened up, new forces have come into play, new tasks are demanding attention — all because Marxism has succeeded in bringing about a new correlation of forces, nationally and internationally, which are acting and reacting on one another...

In other words, the communists have to be better Marxists to solve the present, apparent, crises of Marxism.[15]

---

[15] 'Marxism Today and Tomorrow', editorial in *The Marxist Review*. Calcutta, May-June, 1968, p. 1-3.

NEW CHINA AND SALVATION HISTORY —
A METHODOLOGICAL ENQUIRY

CHOAN-SENG SONG [1]

New China in world history

'In the forty-five years from the 1911 revolution (...) to the present day,
the appearance of China has completely changed. In another forty-five
years, i.e. up to 2001 when we enter into the 21st century, the appearance
of China will change again greatly. China will become a strong socialist
industrial country. That is what China should be. She is a country of
96,000,000 square kilometers, and of 600 million people. She ought to
make a tremendous contribution to humanity. For a long time in the past
her contribution has been meagre and this makes us feel ashamed.'

So writes Mao Tse-tung in 1956 in his article *Chi-nien Sun Chung-shan
hsien-sheng* (in memoriam of Mr Sun Yat-sen).[2]

This is a far-sighted prediction. It was made by a revolutionary visionary
who is firmly rooted in the long history of China, endowed with an uncanny
sense for the future, and the tenacious will to translate the future into
the present. But why has Mao Tse-tung said that China's contribution
to humanity in the past was meagre? Is such a verdict on China's past
true and justified? Is China's civilization, which stands on a par with
the Greco-Roman civilization, or with the civilization of Tigris and
Euphrates, for example, not itself a vast and rich contribution to humanity? Of course Mao deplores the paucity of Chinese civilization from
the standpoint of the socialist revolution he has successfully led and
accomplished. Hence his statement is a statement based on a definite
ideological emphasis which has shaped the foundation of the People's
Republic of China. In fact, he could have gone further and said that
China's contribution to humanity in the past had been negative precisely
because her civilization was instrumental in the enslavement of the

---

[1] Former Principal of Tainan Theological Seminary, Taiwan, and presently Associate
Director of the Secretariat of the Faith and Order Commission, World Council of Churches. This article is a revised version of a paper read at a seminar on Theological Implications of the New China, sponsored by the Lutheran World Federation and *Pro Mundi Vita*,
held in Bastad, Sweden, 29 January - 2 February 1974, and is published with the permis-
sion of the organizers of the seminar.

[2] The article can be found in the *People's Daily*, 13 November 1966. The quotation is taken
from MAO, *Great Lives Observed*, edited by Jerome Ch'en. Englewood Cliffs, New Jersey:
Prentice Hall, Inc., 1969, p. 62.

Chinese people and because it was a civilization dominated by feudalism, semi-colonialism and superstitions.

This verdict on the past provides a clue to what Mao Tse-tung means by China's tremendous contribution to humanity under the mandate of the Chinese Communist Party. Undoubtedly China, in Mao's conviction, will contribute to humanity by universalizing the dictatorship of the proletariat, thus bringing about a world community structured on the vision of a classless society. On the basis of a close relationship between the Chinese Communist revolution and world socialist revolution as he sees it Mao declares : 'No matter what classes, parties or individuals in an oppressed nation join the revolution, and no matter whether they themselves are conscious of the point or understand it, so long as they oppose imperialism, their revolution becomes part of the proletarian-socialist world revolution and they become allies.' [3] Then comes his call to his comrades to become aware of a world role they are expected to play. 'Situated as we are in this day and age', he demands, 'should we not make the appraisal that the Chinese revolution has become a very important part of the world revolution.' [4] Nothing less than this vision of world revolution could have sustained Mao and his fellow revolutionaries through the thick and thin of the Chinese revolution.

It is with this role of New China in world history that we are primarily concerned. Here is something which ought to engage our serious theological attention. From the theological point of view, we are not interested in New China chiefly because of her geo-political impacts on the world. True, since her entry into the family of nations in the winter of 1971 we have been witnessing a radical change in the balance of world powers. This in itself is a fascinating phenomenon. It drives home to us the fact that the reality of international power-politics does not allow us to be complacent about the use of power that affects the political life of the world community. For this very reason theology, or more specifically Christian faith, which has to do not just with a 'spiritual' part of man but with the totality of this spiritual and material being, cannot avoid the need to come to grips with political problems of our day. As Jürgen Moltmann has said, 'Theology serves future freedom in so far as it prepares the way for it in historical criticism, in ideological criticism, and

---

[3] *Selected Works of Mao Tse-tung*, Vol. II, pp. 344.
[4] *Ibid.*, p. 346-7.

finally, in criticism of institutions.' [5] To this we should add 'criticism of power'.[6] It is power, in both its broad and narrow sense, that gets expressed in institutions, organizations, ideologies and even religions. Power is the source of evil as well as of good. And we may speak of degrees of evil or good because of the relative degrees of power possessed by individuals, groups or nations. It follows that the problem of power is not merely a political but also a theological problem. That is why we must be engaged in the critique of the power manifested by New China. It is strange that there has been little theological critique of New China, although many church-related institutions have undertaken the so-called China Study for a number of years with varying degrees of intensity and of professionalism.

Having made this clear, we need to reiterate our assertion that we come to the study of New China from a theological perspective not essentially because China is now a world power to reckon with in the sense, say, that Papua-New Guinea or Monaco or even Sweden is not. Theology cannot be a partisan of power. In fact, theology differs from politics in the narrow sense in that it stands on the side of the powerless; it seeks to wrestle with the hope of the hopeless. Furthermore, it endeavours to discover meaning in the midst of meaninglessness, to identify with the oppressed and to point to the eternal in and beyond the temporal. For this reason, theology knows no national or political boundaries. It is not to be restricted by geographical or racial factors. Nor can it be fettered by ideological or dogmatic chains. And above all, it cannot allow itself to become a servant, a mouthpiece, of the powerful. Theology is a science of faith which seeks particular application of the meaning of the universal in definite and concrete situations.[7] It is the quest of the meaning of the love of God as the latter relates itself to the life of individuals, nations or the world. Theology is thus at once a most free and most rigorous science — free because it is not confined to a narrowly

---

5   JÜRGEN MOLTMANN, 'Toward a Political Hermeneutics', in *New Theology*, No. 6, edited by Martin E. Marty and Dean G. Peerman, Macmillan, 1969, p. 81.

6   Political science used to be concerned primarily with the institutions through which political life is expressed. But there has been increasing emphasis on political science as the study of power and decision-making. It is this fundamental problem of power which should constitute an important subject matter of theology as well as political science. For an account of political science as an academic discipline, cf. *International Encyclopedia of the Social Sciences*, edited by David C. Sills, Macmillan and Free Press, 1968, Vol. 12, p. 283.

7   Wolfhart Pannenberg, for instance, stresses the relation between theology and particular events when he says: 'It belongs to the task of theology to understand all being *(alles Seiende)* in relation to God, so that without God they simply could not be understood. That is what constitutes theology's universality.' *Basic Questions in Theology*, Vol. 1, translated by George H. Kehn. Philadelphia: Fortress Press, 1970, p. 1.

defined area of study and investigation, and rigorous because the application of the meaning of the universal to definite situations cannot be undertaken without scientific fidelity and purity, as T. F. Torrance puts it. According to Torrance, 'Christian dogmatics is the pure science of theology in which, as in every pure science, we seek to discover the fundamental order in the nature of things and to develop basic forms of thought about them as our understanding is allowed to be controlled by them from beyond our individualism'.[8] This points to the importance of maintaining integrity in our theological approach to New China. We can do so only if we make a conscious effort to free ourselves from political power games which tend to predetermine the method and content of our reasoning.

The quest for the theological meaning of New China can perhaps be formulated as follows: *Do we have in New China a challenge to the Gospel of salvation as this Gospel has been interpreted, developed and propagated by Western forms of Christian faith?* If so, then in what way? It seems that this is a critical question which must constitute the centre of our theological investigation of New China. Perhaps this is not the kind of question to which a categorical yes or a categorical no can be given. It is unlike a mathematical question which allows only one correct answer — true or false. Any simplistic answer will invariably prove to be self-defeating and thus unproductive. The question is charged with dialectical tension and pregnant with far-reaching implications. For one thing, it will certainly lead us to rethink seriously the form and content of the language of Christian faith which we have taken for granted within our various Christian traditions and heritages. And it will urge us to re-examine our obedience to the truth which is inherent in the nature of the Gospel. This is a task which should continuously engage the mind of Christians as China gets herself more and more deeply involved in the process of political, social and cultural transformation. All we purport to do in this paper cannot therefore be more than a preliminary contribution to theological methodology which may serve as a tool in our discussion of theological implications of New China.

Just as the Western nations have, under the profound influence of the spirit of the Christian Bible, set the norms of values and consciousness for the Western world and even beyond, New China seems to have

---

[8] T. F. TORRANCE, *Theological Science*. London: Oxford University Press, 1969, p. 338.

the potentiality of radically changing the course of history for future centuries with her socialist ideal of man and society. This cannot but lead us to ask whether we are standing at the threshold of a new era in which New China will play a decisive role in the human quest of the meaning of life. Is the 'salvation' we have seen in New China going to be the norm determining the shape and content of man's search for what it means to be human? Is New China going to be the main instrument in the appearance of a new world order in which the salvation of man is to have its fulfilment?

These questions are not being asked facetiously. They are sober theological questions related to our understanding of the biblical message in specific contemporary situations. After all, this is a matter of how faith can be related to the life we live here and now. It is at this point that the experience of the Exodus, for example, obtains a symbolic significance which can be transported to the experience of New China, especially the experience of the Long March. We say 'symbolic significance' because the historical details and similarities of these two events are not our primary interest. What we witness both in the case of ancient Israel and in the case of New China is the translation of power that lies behind the symbolic meaning of the Exodus into the shaping of the destiny of a nation and of the world. In the words of Kazuhiko Sumiya, 'The track of the gigantic dynamism of world history may now, once more, be "switched over" by the Long March and the thought of Mao Tse-tung, in the same way that the Exodus of Moses was the take-off point that set the direction of cultural development in ancient Israel and on down through two thousand years of European history.' [9] Granted that there is a striking parallel between the Exodus and the Long March, we must be careful not to treat the parallel as something unique in human history. It can be historically substantiated that changes of momentous nature which have altered the direction and orientation of world culture and history are often marked by the exodus experience of charismatic individuals or groups of people. The traumatic experience of Gautama Buddha before his enlightenment is one example. The temptation of Christ in the wilderness is another. In the history of the nations, Caesar crossing the Rubicon comes to our minds. In modern history the crossing of the Atlantic by the Pilgrim Fathers led to the founding of a new nation.

---

[9] KASUHIKO SUMIYA, 'The Long March and the Exodus', in *China and Ourselves*, edited by Bruce Douglass and Ross Terrill. Boston: Beacon Press, 1969, p. 221.

This being true, it is still valid to ask whether New China is destined to play for future world history the role which ancient Israel has played for the past millenia. We wish to make it clear that we cannot be as certain as Kazuhiko Sumiya seems to be. At this stage we should not forestall the answer. Perhaps there will be no answer in the forseeable future. However, it at least sets our theological enquiry into the meaning of New China in the perspective of world history viewed in the light of salvation history.

The quest for a new theological framework

To juxtapose New China and salvation history poses in fact an embarrassing problem for traditional theology. Theology, for the masterminds of Western theological traditions, seldom gets the chance to break out of the Western historical and cultural framework to which the Word of God in the Bible has been made captive. The so-called non-Christian nations and peoples hardly come to the purview of theology proper. Their place in Christian theology, if any, is merely nominal. It is in missiology and missionary operations that they come under the concentrated assault of Christian concern. Even there the central question is not their legitimate place in the history of salvation in the contexts of their history and culture. They are the targets of missionary effort to win men and women for Christ under different denominational banners and colours. Perhaps it is true to say that the sudden interest shown by mission-minded Western Christian groups towards the spiritual welfare of New China in recent years may not be entirely free from a hidden crusaders' mentality carried over from the hey-day of Western missionary expansion. The assumption that any man or any nation, New China not excepted, can be treated as the object of religious conversion is as missiologically false as biblically untenable. This is the subject which should be basic to any talk on the implication of New China for Christian mission.

Be that as it may, it is our observation that Western theology has not been able to develop a theology of history which would provide room for the nations and peoples of the extra-biblical traditions. The framework of Western theological systems simply excludes them from the *oikonomia* of God. At most they only have a negative place in the Western theological framework. A notable example can be found in Cullmann's interpretation of the primitive Christian conception of time and history. The crux of his theology of history is what he calls 'a slender Christline' which constitutes the core of salvation history. Christ, caught in this slender line as its central point, is curtailed in his redemptive dynamic towards all nations. In reply to the critics of his linear concept of salvation history, Cullmann is at pains to stress that the creation-line which comprises everything between heaven and earth and the Christline represented by the election of Israel and the Church converge into one. 'In the New Testament', he writes 'there cannot be, in addition to the Christline of redemption, another and separate God-line of creation. Rather, the redemptive process receives its world-wide significance not only from the broad base of departure and the broad final goal, but also from the universal outreach of the event at the mid-point, the event in which the narrowing reaches its climax precisely for the sake of the redemption of all.' [10]

This sounds plausible enough, but in reality Cullmann makes no compromise with regard to his distinction between redemptive history and secular world history. He just cannot see creation in the light of redemption. For this reason, we do not see the possibility of extending redemption into secular world history in his theology of history. As he states it, 'Since the time of Abraham there has been occurring a course of events which, to be sure, develops outside of the real redemptive history, but which nevertheless has proceeded from it and will again enter into it; indeed, since Christ's death and resurrection it has already begun to enter into it again. The human figures in this process are the Gentiles, that is, precisely those people who do not figure in that development in redemptive history which began with Abraham.' [11] This is a confused statement, to say the least. And the confusion arises from his basic assumption that there are nations and peoples called Gentiles who originally do not have a place at all in the redemptive history.[12] The crucial question is obviously this: Is the salvation history intensely exhibited in both the Old and New Testament to be regarded as the absolute norm whereby events in world history get chosen arbitrarily to be incorporated into God's salvation in Christ, or is it to be looked upon as a pattern or

---

[10] OSCAR CULLMANN, *Christ and Time*, revised edition. Translated by Floyd V. Filson, Philadelphia: Westminster Press, 1964, p. 178.

[11] *Ibid.*, p. 180.

[12] In his *Salvation in History* (London: SCM Press, 1967), Cullmann speaks of the by-passing of events by salvation history: '...In the New Testament salvation-historical perspective which also begins with the creation of the world and ends with the new creation, *a whole period*, so to speak, drops out. In this period things happened which were important to secular history and the history of the Jewish people, but not a single one of them is salvation history for the New Testament' (pp. 157-158).

a type of God's salvation manifested in a massively concentrated way in ancient Israel and in the history of the Church and thus to be discovered in varied degrees of intensity and concentration in other nations and peoples also ? Presumably Cullmann and many Western theologians will take the former position. But we want to argue in the following pages of this paper that it is in the latter position that we will find a new theological framework for our quest of the meaning of nations and peoples, in this case New China, in the salvation of God for the world.

Before developing our thesis put forward above, we need to discuss two theological positions which will have more positive relation to our quest here. One is that of Wolfhart Pannenberg and the other is that of Schubert Ogden. In the theology of Pannenberg, the problem of history and world or universal history receives a disproportionately large amount of attention. This is a welcome change from traditional theological positions such as Cullmann's of which mention has already been made. His basic theological assertion regarding history is as follows : 'History is the most comprehensive horizon of Christian theology. All theological questions and answers are meaningful only within the framework of the history which God has with humanity and through humanity with His whole creation — the history moving toward a future still hidden from the world but already revealed in Jesus Christ.' [13] He thus even speaks of revelation *as* history,[14] namely history taken as a totality, and not just certain events set apart as redemptive history. It is this totality of history which becomes the carrier of God's revelation. On the basis of this thesis, Pannenberg comes upon an important principle of theological hermeneutics for biblical texts. According to him, historical enquiry related to biblical texts must take note of the fact that 'the event sought in inquiring behind the texts does not manifest itself for what it really is when taken as an isolated fact, but does so only within universal continuities of events and of meaning, i.e. only within the horizon of universal history...' [15] Although Pannenberg still needs to make clear what he means by universal history, his hermeneutical principle frees the biblical witness to God's love and salvation from the narrow confinement of the so-called *Heilsgeschichte* solely represented by ancient Israel and by the Christian Church. As Carl Braaten has observed, this 'accent on the universal historical scope of revelation is a new departure in modern

---

[13] PANNENBERG, *op. cit.*, Vol. 1, p. 15.
[14] Cf. *Revelation as History*, edited by Wolfhart Pannenberg, Macmillan, 1968.
[15] PANNENBERG, *Basic Questions in Theology*, Vol. 1, p. 98.

theology. It overcomes the cleavage between salvation history and world history that has been a common feature of both *Heilsgeschichte* and existentialist views of revelation (...). The totality of reality as history is God's world which He creates and through which He reveals Himself. The living God of the Bible is the Lord of the nations, not a local, tribal deity of Israel.' [16] The assertion that God is the Lord of nations is hardly a new theological discovery of Pannenberg. But his merit consists in making the assertion in an effort to do justice to the interrelatedness between God in the Bible and the totality of reality called history.

Having said this, we have to point out that Pannenberg's thesis also presents us with some difficulties. What, for instance, is this total reality called history? Is this not a philosophical abstraction which has no immediate designation with respect to specific events, persons or nations? Furthermore, when Pannenberg stresses the indirect nature of revelation — he rejects the idea of the self-revelation of God [17] — it can be asked whether his concept of revelation means anything at all. For if revelation is still a viable theological concept, is this not to flatten it out in such a way that revelation and history become interchangeable concepts? Moreover, this kind of universalistic language can be dangerous unless it is applied carefully, for it can be a projection of the West-centred Judeo-Christian understanding of history. As a matter of fact, the criticism that his concept of world history smacks of Hegelianism is not entirely wide of the mark.[18] Therefore, despite the fact that Pannenberg has given us a much broader basis of history from which we may understand the biblical concept of revelation, we must not be misled into the situation in which non-Western nations become once again subservient to the mainstream of salvation history. The rise of New China, or Old China for that matter, will certainly invalidate such a theology of history.

If the understanding of revelation and history such as Pannenberg's is to serve any useful purpose at all for our quest of the meaning of New China in salvation history, it must be corrected by the direct relationship between God's acts and historical events. This is to say, God acts in history universally in such a way that historical events in the extra-Jewish/Christian traditions bear direct relationships with the historical

---

[16] CARL E. BRAATEN, *History and Hermeneutics*, New Directions in Theology, Vol. 2. Philadelphia : Westminster Press, 1966, p. 29.

[17] Cf. Pannenberg's Introduction in *Revelation as History*.

[18] Cf. BRAATEN, *op. cit.*, pp. 29-30.

events in the Bible. It is Ogden who expounds very effectively the direct
nature of God's acts in history. That is why what he has to say about
the acts of God will throw some light on our investigation here.

'God's action', according to Ogden, 'is the act whereby, in each new
present, He constitutes Himself as God by participating fully and completely in the world of His creatures, thereby laying the ground for the
next stage of the creative process. Because His love, unlike ours, is pure
and unbounded, His relation to His creatures and theirs to Him is direct
and immediate.' [19] Here the narrow theological norms which Western
theologians have imposed upon their systems are overcome. God
relates Himself directly to all creatures. The affirmation of such a direct
relationship is very crucial because salvation history can no longer be
regarded as an extension or an expansion of the *Heilsgeschichte* conceived
in Western theological terms. Salvation history is present already in the
histories of nations, and in this case, in the history of New China. This
completely nullifies the old concept of Christian mission as the extension
of the Western Christendom. Furthermore, it puts into question the
validity of mission interest currently shown by certain groups of Western
Christians. China might have been lost to the Western churches, but not
to God. To agitate to carry the banner of the Gospel back to China
from the West, is to deny the presence of God in China through His
own acts. By now it is abundantly clear that salvation history is not to
be confused with Western cultural or even moral values. Not even
Western technological developments are destined to bring happiness to
mankind. Increasingly, ecologists are telling us that the opposite may
well be the case.

Does this mean that all theological judgment is now to be suspended
and that all historical events will be identified with the acts of God for
man's salvation? Not at all. For to say that all historical events are
God's acts is as meaningless as to say history as such is God's revelation,
as we pointed out earlier in our discussion of Pannenberg's theology.
As a matter of fact, in every sphere of human activity a certain principle
of selection is operative. This is true in scientific research in which data
are weighed and shifted in such a way that many factors get eliminated as
irrelevant or even harmful. This is no less true in our own personal life,
in our relationships with our fellow creatures, in our search for the
meaning and destiny of history. As Ogden has pointed out, 'Some of

---

[19] SCHUBERT OGDEN, *The Reality of God*. London : SCM Press, 1967, p. 177.

our outer acts of word and deed either are in fact or at least are understood to be *our* acts in a way that others are not. Because certain of our actions give peculiarly apt expression to what we are (...), these actions *are* our actions (or are believed to be our actions) in a special sense.' [20] This is an important observation which is of particular relevance to a theological critique of history. If Christians or theologians feel called upon to bear prophetic witness to the events of history, they will forfeit their call if they resort to a wholesale acceptance or rejection of the events concerned. The prophets in the Old Testament stand out as the conscience of the nation precisely because of the cutting edge which their pronouncements on personal, national and world events displayed. It is this 'prophetic cutting edge' which is very much needed in our theological attempt to understand the meaning of the complexity of the current international politics and to make sense of the salvation out of New China.

In line with the above consideration, Ogden establishes an important theological criterion to deal with the relationship between God's acts and events in history. According to him, 'wherever or in so far as an event in history manifests God's characteristic action as Creator and Redeemer, it actually is His act in a sense in which other historical events are not.' [21] Here is the clue to the answer to the baffling question: 'What do you mean by God acting in history?' God's acts are not to be regarded as supernatural intervention which bears only tangential relation with the stuff of our life and history. They constitute the texture of history. That is why Christ refused to set our hope on the Kingdom of God conceived as supra-historical. Asked by the Pharisees when the Kingdom of God was coming, Christ replied: 'The Kingdom of God is not coming with signs to be observed; nor will they say, "Lo, here it is!" or "There!" for behold, the Kingdom of God is in the midst of you.' [22] We therefore find ourselves in agreement with Ogden when he further says: 'What is meant when we say that God acts *in* history is primarily that there are certain distinctively human words and deeds in which His characteristic action as Creator and Redeemer is appropriately represented or revealed.' [23] By human words and deeds Ogden does not mean only the words and deeds represented and revealed in

---

[20] *Ibid.*, p. 182.

[21] *Ibid.*

[22] Luke 17 : 20-21.

[23] OGDEN, *op. cit.*, p. 184.

ancient Israel and in the formation of the Christian Church. They can be also the words and deeds of man anywhere and anytime ; for according to him, the 'capacity to discern meaning and to give it symbolic expressions is what lies behind the whole complex phenomenon of human culture'.[24] It is this human capacity that has been relegated to limbo by some neo-orthodox theologians in contemporary theology. This theological trend, together with the other-worldly emphasis of fundamentalism, has not enabled the churches in Asia to read the handwritings on the wall of Asian politics. The radical shift in world politics brought about by the emergence of New China has exposed the complacency of Asian churches under the tutelage of the churches in the West. It also challenges them to reinterpret the meaning of salvation history in the new and complex historical contexts. In dealing with the phenomenon of New China, Christian theology will need a set of new biblical and theological assumptions that will provide fresh insights into the acts of God in the extra-biblical histories.

New China in salvation history

As we have mentioned earlier, the importance of New China for our theological consideration stems from the realization that she will play a crucial role in the future course of world history. The impact she will have on the world is not to be restricted to politics in the narrow sense of the word, but on the meaning and shape of human life which man is after by various means and ways, including religion. In other words, here is a pattern and shape of life which proposes to offer the ultimate to the truth for which man searches and therefore claims to replace all other searches for the truth related to man and the world. As Stuart Schram has said, to the extent that Mao Tse-tung 'sees China as the only genuinely socialist great power — the Soviet Union having definitely taken the road of revisionism and the restoration of capitalism — the ideological purity and firmness of will of the Chinese revolutionaries is henceforth the principal guarantee of ultimate victory on a world scale'.[25] Indeed, New China as a great socialist power poses a threat to other social and political systems, especially that of the West. It is no wonder that the West, chiefly represented by the United States, first sought to destroy it. Having failed to destroy it, the United States resorted to

---

[24] *Ibid.*, p. 181.
[25] STUART SCHRAM, *Mao Tse-tung*. Penguin Books Ltd., revised edition, 1967, p. 321.

the strategy of containment. When even this did not bring about the desired result, she began to engage herself in *détente* with it.

But will this new strategy succeed in curbing the messianic role which New China has taken upon herself with regard to the future and destiny of mankind ? Political *détente* based on *realpolitik* may bring about a fragile structure of peace. Although it is a question whether such a structure will stand the test of future international crises, it certainly is not capable of facing the spiritual force at work in New China to change the face of the earth. What New China envisages to accomplish on a world scale will affect the texture not only of human society but of human beings. According to Ross Terrill, the Chinese Communist Party 'does not think of socialism as ending with the building of socialism in China. They expect revolution eventually to bring about socialism all over the world. They believe it is to be their right and duty to assist, however indirectly, these revolutionary transformations.' [26] In the complex power play of our present world, the leadership which China purports to exercise beyond her borders will not always find unquestioned acceptance. The failure of Communist transformation in Indonesia is an example. But the socialist movement pressing for the rights of the oppressed, the poor and the powerless will go on, and China will continue to be a major physical and spiritual force behind the movement.

It is at this point that a link between New China and salvation history can be established. Salvation history in the sense of God's acts in history is intensely acted out in the transition of the old China to the New China and in the continuing effort of the Chinese Communist Party to transform man and his society. Again, reference to the Exodus will serve as both a useful comparison and a point of departure. In the theocratic society of ancient Israel God's acts in the history of the Israelites and their neighbouring nations are expressed in religious contexts. Moses went down to Egypt to lead his people out of bondage in the name of Yahweh, the God of his fathers. His mission of the Exodus is therefore preceded by his call through an intense spiritual experience in the wilderness on Horeb. He is instructed by Yahweh to confront his people in Egypt and the house of Pharaoh in the name of 'I AM ; that is who I am'. [27]

This pattern of call, intense spiritual struggle and the divine self-identification becomes the axis around which the mission of deliverance is

---

[26] *China Profile, A Symposium*, edited by Ross Terrill. New York : Friendship Press, 1969, pp. 145-146.
[27] Exodus 3 : 13-14.

carried out in the Old Testament. In this sense, the prophets such as Isaiah, Jeremiah and even the unknown prophet designated as the Second Isaiah are all true to the Mosaic tradition. The same thing can be said of Jesus Christ too. His temptation in the wilderness marks the end of His life as a private religious person and signals the beginning of His mission of salvation. Questioned by His adversaries about the authority with which He says and does things differently, He points beyond Himself to God with whose cause He has completely identified Himself. He is reported to have said : 'In truth, in very truth I tell you, the Son can do nothing by Himself; He does only what He sees the Father doing ; what the Father does, the Son does.' [28] Salvation history in the Bible thus demonstrates most clearly that it is God who acts in history through certain nations and especially through certain personalities. To put it differently, in the Bible history is interpreted redemptively not because it is different in substance from the so-called secular history but because it is seen as the arena of God's activity through man as His agent. And in the case of the biblical traditions the man called upon to read the divine activity out of the stuff of history is deeply conscious of being under the power and authority of God. For him, history is nothing apart from God.

What we have in New China is a secularized version of salvation history. It is no less salvation history because its basic ideological thrust is that of atheistic materialism. It would not even be quite right theologically to say that New China serves as a negative example to salvation history because of her determination to do away with religions. In fact, she has proved herself to be an extreme case of the theology of secularity carried to its logical conclusion. She is a telling example of how man can do without a hypothesis called God or a *deus ex machina*. In the hands of the Chinese Communist Party, the land of many gods and many lords has been completely de-sacralized. In this process of de-sacralization which culminated in the Cultural Revolution, Christianity, along with other religions, suffered a crashing blow. And out of this de-sacralizing process Mao Tse-tung and his thought have come to fill the vacuum left by the defeat of many gods and many lords. New China has thus emerged as a formidable spiritual force and institution contesting for supremacy against other spiritual forces and institutions represented by the time-honoured great world religions.

---

[28] John 5 : 19.

This bears a strong stamp of the prophetic activity in the Bible. The prophets in ancient Israel have the whole history of the nation to contend with. They have to uncover the extortion and injustice committed against the powerless by the powerful, against the poor by the rich, and against the masses by the political élite. The eighth-century prophet Isaiah does not mince his words when he addresses himself to the social evils of his day:

> 'Shame on you! You who make unjust laws and publish burdensome decrees, depriving the poor of justice, robbing the weakest of my people of their rights, despoiling the widow and plundering the orphan.' [29]

Social conflicts have reached such an intensity that nothing short of revolution seems to be able to bring Israel back to the nation in which the justice of God prevails. What is described here is a society courting a revolution. But salvation history in Israel took a different course than that in China. The prophets proved to be the conscience of the nation but not the revolutionaries of a new social order. It was in her inter-action with foreign political powers that the ancient Israel experienced a revolution of immense magnitude which gave her a unique place in salvation history. Thus, she became a supreme pattern of how God's judgment and salvation are at work in the world of nations.

The message of Jesus too bears a strangely proletarian character. It must be said with great regret that His message has undergone adultera-tion in the Western capitalist society. Those passages which speak for the underprivileged are interpreted spiritually to give false comfort to the poor and give rise to complacent justification for the rich. But it has become crystal clear that the masses in the Third World, and particularly the awakened masses in New China, will no longer put up with this kind of spiritualization. The revolution of the masses poses an unprecedented challenge to the Church not to evade the issues contained in some sayings of Jesus. The Lukan version of the Sermon on the Mount, for example, as it is rendered by the New English Bible, leaves not the slightest doubt as to its down-to-earth implications:

> 'How blessed are you who are in need; the Kingdom of God is yours.
> How blessed are you who now go hungry; your hunger shall be satisfied.
> How blessed are you who weep now; you shall laugh.'

---

[29] Isaiah 10:1-2.

This blessing to the poor is immediately followed by His condemnation of the rich. His language is explicit and unequivocal :

'But alas for you who are rich ; you have had your time of happiness.
Alas for you who are well-fed now ; you shall go hungry.
Alas for you who laugh now ; you shall mourn and weep.' [30]

Is Jesus then a social revolutionary ? In recent years there has been a strong trend in radical Christian circles to claim Jesus as such. But it is doubtful whether this can be fully substantiated biblically. In the story of the temptation He is depicted as rejecting the purely political means of solving the problems of the deeply troubled world of mankind. He goes about teaching and practising love instead of hate. He refuses to have anything to do with division of property. And finally He submits Himself to the power from which His own people longed to be emancipated.

It would be wrong, however, to conclude from this that Jesus has no interest whatsoever in a new social order. During the short span of His ministry, what He endeavours to bring about is a revolution of a radical kind. As He sees it, a new social order, or the Kingdom of God here and now, must be based on man's complete re-orientation. Man must be freed from preoccupation with himself and turn to God, who is the Creator and Redeemer. When his alienation from God is overcome, his alienation from his fellow man will also be overcome. The tragedy is that Christianity has, over the centuries, institutionalized the healing that takes place between God and man with the result that the healing of alienation at the personal and interpersonal level has been rendered ineffective. And when Christianity becomes captive to the Western capitalist society, the Christian mission cannot but turn out to be the charity of the rich towards the poor, and the sympathy of the privileged towards the less privileged. As Neale Hunter has aptly remarked, 'The final irony was that Christianity, a religion based on the Incarnation, was rejected by the Chinese as an extreme form of *alienation*. This has been interpreted as an unqualified "No !" to the Gospel, but if we look close we see that it was really a rejection of a particular kind of theology, of a theology that represented nineteenth-century Christianity's massive denial of its own theological roots and its profound compromise with the philosophical underpinnings of capitalism.' [31] Christianity in the process

---

[30] Luke 6 : 20-25.
[31] NEALE HUNTER, 'The Good News and the Good Society', in *China and Ourselves*, pp. 174-188, p. 182.

of its historical development may have alienated the masses of the Chinese people caught in an unprecedented socialist transformation ; it must be said with all emphasis that Jesus has not. Jesus Himself lived and died for God and for man, and He believes that a new social order will come into being when men and women have learnt to live for God and for one another.

It is in the light of Jesus Christ, and not on the basis of the Western version of historical Christianity, that we can begin to see the profound meaning of God's acts in New China. The order that now prevails in New China seems to reflect partially the order which God has brought into being out of chaos and disorder. The land which used to be torn and laid waste by natural disasters and by man's inhumanity and brutality has begun to function again for the welfare of the Chinese population. And the society in which fear and darkness dominated seems to assume its constructive role again for its members. The *tohu wabohu* of the war of resistance against Japan and the civil war is now a thing of the past. New China seems now destined to represent the possibility of a future classless society in which the dictatorship of the proletariat will prevail completely. Supreme confidence in achieving this ultimate goal is reflected in Mao Tse-tung's poem 'Chingkanshan Revisited', written in 1965, which runs partly as follows :

> 'Thirty-eight years have elapsed
> Like a snap of the fingers.
> Reach the ninth heaven high to embrace the moon
> Or the five oceans deep to capture a turtle : either is possible.
> Return to merriment and triumphant songs.
> Under this heaven nothing is difficult,
> If only there is the will to ascend.' [32]

Is this not a picture of man come of age ? Has New China under the leadership of Mao Tse-tung found the way to shape the destiny of a nation or even of the world for the welfare of the majority of people ?

The freedom to be human

To use the language of Christian faith, is New China the Kingdom of God realized ? Does she find the way to salvation in the fullest sense of the word ? It is to questions such as these that we will turn in this last part of our discussion.

---

[32] *Mao*, edited by Jerome Ch'en, p. 113.

Let us begin by stating clearly that New China is not the realized King-dom of God. This must be stressed in spite of her social, economic and political achievements, in spite of the new social order in which the suffering of the masses is largely eliminated, and in spite of new ethical purity brought about by discipline and ascetism. Mao Tse-tung himself will deny any equation of New China and the Kingdom of God, even if the latter is interpreted in its secular meaning and as having nothing to do with the utopia of religious illusion. That is why he has contrived to make revolution into a permanent institution. It seems as if revolu-tion has acquired an inertia which transforms the internal struggles within the Chinese Communist Party and the external pressures from interna-tional power politics into predictable regularity. 'Among Mao's contri-butions to Marxist-Leninist theory and practice', observes Donald Mac-Innis, 'is the doctrine (...) of permanent revolution — or revolution within revolution. Continuing "struggle" as the agent of internal change — for individuals, for the society, for the nation — has directed the durable Chinese leader's strategy at every stage of the Communist revo-lution, including the present.' [33] Here we seem to have an eschatological tension of 'already' and 'not yet'. This is the future of hope at once realized and suspended in the present.

But we are not quite certain whether this eschatological tension is a genuine philosophical principle serving the vision of a classless utopia or a revolutionary strategy to consolidate the power of the party leadership. The latter seems to be the case if permanent revolution is seen against the background of the absolutist political structure of New China. The intense power struggle that is still going on within the top party leader-ship even after the fall of Lin Piao, once the heir-designate to Mao Tse-tung, seems to be indicative of this.[34] A close look at the mass-line which underlines Mao's revolutionary theory and practice may therefore be theologically significant. There is no question about the fact that no one has read the mind of the masses of Chinese people more accurately than Mao Tse-tung. He sums up his deep insight in the now famous

[33] DONALD E. MACINNIS, 'A New Man and a New Society', in *China, the Peasant Revolu-tion*, WSCF Books, Vol. 2, No. 1, 1972. Serial No. 4. London : F. I. Litho Ltd., p. 17.

[34] Jürgen Domes concludes his leading article, 'A Rift in the New Course', in *Far Eastern Economic Review*, 1 October 1973, by saying : 'Besides the problem of individual successors to the Chairman, the even greater problem of successors to the old revolu-tionary élite is still wide open. Even after the Tenth Congress, nobody can tell what kind of persons with what kind of a world outlook are going to rule China in the 1980s. Only one thing is sure : a new major policy dispute has become clear since early 1973, and it began to surface at the Congress. This dispute could lead to a new deep rift in Chinese domestic politics within the next two or three years.'

metaphorical statement: 'Our God is none other than the masses of Chinese people.' Perhaps the year 1949 which brought the Communist Party to power in China can be seen as the beginning of a subtle change in the place and function of the mass-line in the continuing revolution. Before 1949 Mao Tse-tung and his fellow revolutionaries identified themselves with the masses to win liberation from the Japanese invasion and to come out of the civil war as victor. What was at stake in that long period of struggle was the survival and the destiny of the nation as a whole. There would be no future for China unless she was liberated from imperialism, feudalism and superstition. It was this liberation which the Communist Party was able to bring to the masses of Chinese People in 1949. But this momentous event also marked the end of revolution against external enemies. A new era of the consolidation of power thus began. The dynamics of the masses is now released at appropriate times to combat revisionism and to bring downfall upon those who dare to challenge Mao. The masses are organized and institutionalized to serve the absolutist political system of which Mao Tse-tung is the personification.

The following poem composed by a girl in praise of Mao gives a glimpse of the totalitarian framework which shapes the life and thought of men and women in China today:

'If you do not study Chairman Mao's writing for a day,
The food will not taste good and the night will be unsleepable.
If you do not study Chairman Mao's writing for two days,
You will feel as though your eyes are being covered with scales.
If you do not study Chairman Mao's writing for three days,
You will be lost in direction and your mind will be dim.' [35]

The Incarnation is God's freedom to be human. In Jesus Christ God has shown what it means to be human. To be human, as Jesus demonstrated in life and in death, is to be open to God and to man. Openness is thus an essential nature of humanness. The story of the fall in the third chapter of Genesis conveys to us this basic truth about the relationship between man's openness and his humanness as essential components of salvation. The fall consists in the fact that man has lost his openness to God and to his fellow man. He must hide from God, and he must accuse his fellow companion for his own protection. Thus salvation

---

[35] Cf. DONALD E. MACINNIS, *Religious Policy and Practice in Communist China*. Macmillan, 1972, Doc. 90, p. 287.

consists in reopening the channel of communication with God and with other human creatures. In Jesus Christ the restoration of communication has taken place. He is a man for God and for other human beings. The New Testament writers are at pains to use different images to tell us how negation of absolutism and rejection of authoritarianism become the essential parts of salvation in Christ. There is the manger in which Jesus lay when He was born. In His entry into Jerusalem He rode on an ass, a very humble creature. And He chose the cross to end His life and work. When we come to Paul's letters, we discover that he frequently uses the term *dulos*, meaning literally slave, to identify his relationship with Christ. Furthermore in the New Testament obedience is stressed as an essential part of Christian discipleship.

Because of the use of images and concepts such as these, there has been persistent objection to Christian faith as religion for the weak, as a defeatist kind of faith, which has no positive meaning for modern man. Such criticism of the Christian faith is based on a misunderstanding of the meaning of these images and concepts. What these images and concepts primarily intend to aim at is not the humiliation of man. They are not meant to foster in the believers negativism and passivity towards life and the world. The truth is that they are intended to reject the kind of power that creates barriers among people and refuses to recognize the acts of God in history. They point to the depth of man's being where the spirit of communion can be genuinely expressed in the act of inter-personal communication. In other words, they are meant to stress man's openness towards God and towards other human beings as inseparable from salvation, namely, from being truly human.

We have to admit that the power exercised in an absolutist political state alienates a man from God and from his fellow man. Concentration of such power results therefore in intensification of alienation. It follows that disclosure of one's self to other people becomes severely restricted and even distorted. In this kind of situation people are prone to treat each other at a less human level. When one central power dominates and dictates what a person should think, say and act, which seems to be the case in New China and is certainly the case in other nations under the totalitarian form of government, he cannot but find himself limited in his freedom to be truly human. He cannot be as open to his fellow man as he would like to be. He is denied openness in expressing his spiritual needs and longings in ways other than those prescribed by the political authorities. Hence, Donald MacInnis concludes his documentary history of religious policy and practice in Communist China with the following observation: 'On the one hand, the record of these past twenty years shows a consistent adherence to orthodox Marxist dogma on religion in all theoretical analyses and doctrinal statements, while holding to the equally consistent adherence in official statements and theoretical discussions to the constitutional guarantee of freedom of religious belief; yet in practice, with some ambivalence from period to period, religious believers have suffered increasing constraints on the practice of their faith down to the total suppression of open religious activity by Red Guard militants in 1966-67.' [36]

When an ideology becomes coupled with the dogmatism of political power, as in the case of Marxism, it can easily become an absolute norm and criterion imposed on the totality of life. When the people of Israel passed from the period of nomadic wandering and fighting for existence into the nation structured under the power of the monarch, a similar kind of ideological rigidity set in. It was the indomitable spirit of the prophets which challenged it and fought it. Could we expect to see this kind of prophetic spirit arise in the future to assert the freedom of the spirit in a socialist-communist state such as China?

The acts of God in China which have taken the revolutionary movement of liberation from poverty, starvation and exploitation will now perhaps manifest themselves in the struggle for the freedom of the spirit. The drama of salvation history in China in the days ahead will therefore be the drama of the human spirit fighting for the freedom to be human.

Salvation is the freedom to be human. It cannot be achieved without the freedom of the spirit. As Berdyaev put it so well: 'Freedom cannot be the result of compulsion, even of the harmonized perfected order of living: this very order must be the result of freedom. Salvation comes from the Truth which gives us freedom, but compulsory salvation is impossible and unnecessary. Man's salvation cannot be achieved without man's freedom. Salvation is man's liberation in Truth, in God.' [37] It may not be entirely wishful thinking to hope that God, the Creator and the Redeemer, will chart the course of salvation history in China in such a way that the masses of Chinese people who found liberation from the evils of the old society may yet find liberation in truth and in God. All

---

[36] *Ibid.*, p. 373.

[37] *Christian Existentialism*, a Berdyaev Anthology, selected and translated by Donald A. Lowrie. London: George Allen and Unwin Ltd., 1965, p. 139.

this goes to show that New China, just as other nations in the past and also in the future, is part of the salvation history which begins with the old creation and ends with the new. She is therefore an integral part of the creation which, according to the Apostle Paul, 'will be set free from its bondage to decay and obtain the glorious liberty of the children of God'.[38]

---

[38] Romans 8 : 21.

LIBERATION FOR SOCIAL JUSTICE

The Common Struggle of Christians and Marxists in Latin America

JULIO DE SANTA ANA [1]

From out of many different contexts in Latin America voices can be heard emphasizing that the achieving of a new, just society must involve a profound transformation of our peoples, not only in terms of economic, social and political patterns but also in our cultural values and personal styles of behaviour. Such a process implies the breaking down of existing situations of economic dependence and political oppression in order that people may come to stand on their own feet. This is what is meant by the word 'liberation' : a symbol by which Latin Americans point to the goal towards which we are striving. Our struggle has of course its own specific context and characteristics, and these have also shaped the changes in relationship between Christians and Marxists over the last twenty years.

In contrast to what happened in Europe in the same period, the dialogue between Christians and Marxists in Latin America was not mainly academic in character ; it resulted from the meeting and collaboration of persons who, though differing in their views of the world and of life itself, were engaged in joint action. This phenomenon has not, of course, affected the whole Christian community, let alone all Marxist groups, but it is a trend which is spreading with increasing rapidity. What only fifteen years ago was regarded by many as the fad of a few is now too common to be overlooked. Admittedly, it prompts passionate reactions for or against. These in turn imply the adoption of a political standpoint. For in Latin America Christianity and Marxism are not so much intellectual views as expressions of forces which dynamically affect reality. In an extremely volatile context whose various elements are constantly shifting position, Christianity and Marxism repeatedly intersect, by no means always in the same way. While it is possible to observe a certain constancy in Marxist standpoints, the same cannot be said of the way Christians express themselves. It is still the case that there are large sectors of society calling themselves Christian (it would be more appropriate to say that they invoke a Christian tradition) and who reject

[1] Dr DE SANTA ANA, of Uruguay, was formerly Secretary of ISAL (Church and Society in Latin America), and is now Secretary for Studies of the WCC Commission on the Churches' Participation in Development (CCPD).

Marxism. But others, increasingly numerous, are now using Marxist elements in their analysis and understanding of the situation, while yet others are openly joining movements in which Marxists take the lead.

From mutual anathema to joint endeavour

In the first half of this century the two forces were in flat contradiction. Christians, Catholics above all, saw in Marxism an active agent of social change which would have disastrous consequences for Latin American society, in whose development the Catholic Church had played a fundamental part. The ideological artillery of Catholic preaching was brought into action first against socialism, then against communism too. In face of the possible entry of Marxist atheism on the Latin American scene, it was urgent for the Church to encourage various specialized movements of apostolic action: among industrial workers, intellectuals, young people, and so on. At that time Marxism was considered to be totally incompatible with Christian faith. The Protestant minority in Latin America held a similar if less virulent view. At that time Protestantism appeared as an agent of modernization for Latin America. Yet despite its greater ability to understand the urgency of social justice in a society which suffered enormous disparities and contradictions, it could not accept Marxism as a legitimate element. For Christians, then, Marxism must be opposed and driven out.

The Marxists, for their part, regarded Christianity (above all Roman Catholicism) as the traditional ally of those who had prevented the social progress of the people, a tool by which the minorities who had always governed Latin America had been able to domesticate the mass of the people and consolidate their oppressive power. For Marxists, the Church was a power to be fought; Christian faith was an element to be rooted out from the minds of the people. Each side was thus anathema to the other. The contradictions were deep and tense. Reconciliation and dialogue were impossible.

Nevertheless, in the course of the 1950s, the situation began to change. More and more, especially in the universities, Marxists and Christians were to be found united in a common struggle against injustice (until very recently university students played an important role in the social struggles of Latin America). Though at first this was a cause of astonishment to both sides, both became passionately interested in studying the motives and methods involved. A cautiously receptive attitude began to replace rigid anathema. Little by little some Marxists began to detect an element which until then they had not perceived in Christianity : a basic good-will seeking to express the love which faith preaches.

Legitimate allies

For Christians this open attitude to Marxism implied, at least at that time, three things : first, the recognition of Marxists as legitimate allies in the struggle for social change; second, an interest in Marxism, its doctrinal bases and political views, which had earlier been rejected *a priori*; third, acquaintance with a method of analysis which could provide a more complete knowledge of the Latin American situation. On the other hand, the same process led the Marxists to understand how much closer the Christians were to the Latin American masses ; to realize that however alienating some Christian ideas might be (chiefly because of the way in which they had been manipulated by the ruling classes), they were nevertheless integral to the level of consciousness reached by the Latin American peoples ; and to realize that even if in the social as well as in the political sphere Marxism is the conception which best suits the legitimate interests of the masses, Marxists should not simply reject all that is Christian but should seek to know it better.

For Christians, whether through the *aggiornamento* promoted by John XXIII among Catholics or through the attitudes that the ecumenical movement brought to Latin American Protestantism, the *rapprochement* with Marxism warmed up in the 1960s. Groups of Catholics and Protestants gradually became convinced that the cause of the great ills of Latin America lay, as the Marxists said, in economic imperialism. By applying a Marxist analysis to Latin American reality, many Christians came to understand that the actions of economic imperialism had subordinated our nations to the system of exploitation imposed on all the underdeveloped nations.[2] This, of course, was nothing new for Latin American Marxists. The important thing was that on the basis of this conviction Christians and Marxists began to agree about the need to overcome this state of affairs by a process of change described as *liberation*. In a document produced by an ecumenical group we read the following :

> 'The question is not so much how to describe our dependence or establish which are the groups that maintain it, as to ask how it is to be overcome. This victory will not be produced by any miracle, nor through the inexorable

---

[2] Cf. *América Latina, Movilización Popular y Fé Cristiana*. Montevideo : ISAL, 1971, p. 140.

and magical process of history. In order to overcome our situation of dependence, we must encourage the organization of those sectors of the people which are exploited by the dominant classes of the nations and by imperialism. (...) For these political groups, liberation from dependence by an efficient revolutionary method necessarily implies the working out of a strategy (which in turn implies the adoption of a specific political thesis which must be translated into a theory of change) and decision about the tactical steps to be carried out according to an established set of priorities. We must understand that this strategy and tactics has to take fundamental account of the historical reality of each country, profiting by experiences gained in other places without making them patterns to follow, which always produces alienation. Why a process of liberation in Latin America? Because in order to create a juster society, without odious class distinctions, a more rational organization of production must be established, obeying the actual needs of the workers. It will be a society in which power must be exercised by the classes which at present are being exploited. For this, it will be necessary to socialize the means of production and to make the exercise of power democratic. It will be a new society in which the social will predominate over the individual.' [3]

This document, only one example among many produced during the last five years, shows that the *rapprochement* between Christians and Marxists led to a programme of action in which no fundamental differences separated them. It is as if two currents were now flowing together in a single surging river. Christians and Marxists had in fact come to a similar decision: they were prepared to serve the cause of the oppressed classes in order to establish true justice. This, of course, amounted to a revolutionary decision, in view of the present state of affairs in Latin America. It was not an agreement on merely transitory or accidental matters, but on the goals of action. For many Christians and Marxists, therefore, the time of anathema was long since over. The moment of common action and commitment had come. Fidel Castro, Prime Minister of Cuba, noting this fact, pointed out during his tour of Chile in November 1971 that between Christians and Marxists there was a fundamental alliance, because even if they do not agree about tactics, they do about strategy: 'We must see Christians of the Left, revolutionary Christians, as strategic allies of the revolution — not as fellow-travellers.' He added a call for unity between Marxist and Christian revolutionary forces, and rejected the attitude of exclusion which either might adopt: 'Revolution is the art of combining forces in order to wage decisive battles against imperialism. No revolution can afford the luxury of excluding or despis-

---

[3] *Ibid.*, pp. 143-144.

ing any forces ; no revolution can afford the luxury of excluding the term "to join forces".' [4]

These words of Fidel Castro correspond to observed fact. At the end of the 1950s an occasional priest and a few laymen had taken a decision in favour of revolution. With the passage of time, however, it was now no longer a question of rare individual cases, but of an increasingly strong trend. In fact, in the last ten years a very large number of different movements have sprung up from the churches to espouse the cause of liberation. ISAL came into existence in 1962, and before long took the decision in favour of revolution. The student movements — *Juventud Universitaria Católica* (Catholic University Youth) and *Movimiento Estudiantil Cristiano* (the Student Christian Movement) — were consolidated between 1962 and 1966. The workers' and agrarian movements made a revolutionary option about the year 1966. Independent communities of Christians committed to the revolution were organized from 1962 onward. The first groups of priests working for political aims started in 1967 in Brazil and then developed rapidly in Argentina, Peru, Colombia, Venezuela, etc., the best known being the one which provided the nucleus of 'Christians for Socialism' in Chile, created in 1970.

Open to collaboration

So far we have been speaking only of the Christians. Among the Marxists, various communist and socialist parties and others of Marxist inspiration opened themselves to collaboration with Christians from 1964 onwards. The action of Fr Camilo Torres spurred many of them to make contact with Christians. And so in Chile, Uruguay and Peru, various Marxist political groups openly declared their intention of joining forces with the Christians, not only on the electoral but also on the parliamentary and political levels.

Now common action does not always make it possible to eliminate points of disagreement or to open the way to complete understanding. But in this joint action of Christians and Marxists the disagreements which may exist or the points on which total clarity has not yet been reached are not regarded as insuperable obstacles. Both understand that their dialogue has to do more with practical action and less with abstraction and theory. It is reflection on action which unites, rather than on the points which

---

[4] *Cuba-Chile. Encuentro Simbólico entre dos Procesos Históricos.* Havana : Commission of Revolutionary Orientation of the Central Committee of the Communist Party of Cuba, 1972, pp. 268-278.

still divide, that is important. Such reflection has clearly shown that the Christians have not made a revolutionary choice merely in order to have a place in the society which will follow the revolutionary process, and that the Marxists do not intend merely to manipulate, dominate or use the Christians as a pretext. In the end, it is action which makes it possible to discover what are the real motives and intentions operative in a process of political change. Indeed, this dialogue can only take place in the course of the struggle, fundamentally because the context of their action is one of conflict. In the common struggle, the unsolved problems which opposed Marxism and Christianity cannot divide ; our standpoints, our views of the world and of life may be different, but we respect one another and seek agreement wherever possible.

The realization that the basic reality which we face is one of conflict (class struggle, ideological struggle, etc.) poses such a huge question for Christians and Marxists that it compels them to overcome any residue of sectarianism or dogmatism. What is primary now is, therefore, funda-mental agreement about the aims to be achieved. As those who took part in the meeting of Christians for Socialism (Santiago de Chile, April 1972) said :

> 'The central and inescapable objective of the strategic alliance is to destroy the capitalist system and to combat imperialism. The historical task assumed by the working class (industrial workers and peasants) is the socialist revolution, with the social appropriation of the means of pro-duction and the exercise of power by the working class.
>
> '(. . .) The immediate objective of the strategic alliance between Christians and Marxists is the political awakening and organization of the people ; to enable them to realize in the most fundamental way their exploited condition, and to become aware of their right to be free, even to the point of envisaging the urgent need to seize power.' [5]

Those who took part in that meeting had to face the problem of the specific contribution of Christians to the alliance with Marxists, and they answered it by formulating five points : 1. revolutionary commit-ment, a consequence of taking the part of the oppressed and of sharing their liberating struggle against exploitation ; 2. their own Christian faith, understood in the context of the revolutionary option as 'an insur-rectional consciousness'.[6] By this, the revolutionary Christian can help

---

[5] *Cristianos por el Socialismo.* Santiago de Chile: Mundo Nuevo, 1972, p. 254. See also *Christians and Socialism: Documentation of the Christians for Socialism Movement in Latin America.* Maryknoll, N.Y.: Orbis, 1975.

[6] Ibid., p. 255.

to unmask the forms in which 'capitalism, with its ideology of domination, is camouflaged in a sociological Christianity'[7]; 3. the struggle against a policy which has been that of the churches in Latin America and which suits the mechanisms of domination over the people employed by the ruling classes. On this plane it is a question of ensuring that the Church is really the Church, without losing its identity through the alienation to which the capitalist system may subject it; 4. to ensure that the Christian community lives the renewing and truly revolutionary meaning of faith. For the alliance to be effective, the true identity of men and women of faith must be maintained and communities of revolutionary Christians formed ; 5. to unmask the way capitalism manipulates what is Christian, and at the same time to make the Church aware of the capitalist structure which confines it and which it must overcome in order to stand faithful in the urgency of that love of the neighbour, and especially of the poorest, which Jesus Christ demands.

A new understanding

What specific contributions can Marxists make in their turn in the strategic alliance with Christians ? The Santiago meeting suggested :

> 'The chief contribution of Marxists is their revolutionary experience, their method of work and their firm roots in popular sectors.
> In many Marxist achievements (such as the workers' movements in several countries, the Cuban revolution, etc.), Christians recognize their own aspirations towards a new society and a new man.
> The disinterested struggle for the proletariat which many Marxists engage in enables Christians to discover the grace of love and obliges them to a secularization and purification of faith.
> The political practice of Marxists demands greater political maturity of Christians, for good intentions are not enough.
> Marxism makes it possible for Christians to achieve a new understanding of their history (cf. F. Engel's introduction to K. Marx's *The Class Struggles in France*, 1848 to 1850, 6 March 1895).'[8]

It is evident that joint action challenges Christians and Marxists to mutual change and adjustment. For Christians, in the first place, the revolutionary option involves giving primacy to revolutionary action. If there are some for whom faith loses its importance, it must also be recognized that there are other believers in Jesus Christ who enrich and

---

[7] *Ibid.*, p. 257.
[8] *Ibid.*, pp. 258-259.

discover their faith in this priority accorded to revolution. Secondly, the alliance with the Marxists leads to a change in the consciousness of the Christians who detach themselves from bourgeois values and accept the imperatives of action for liberation.

As for the Marxists, alliance with the Christians is something which challenges them first to be more faithful in their action to the objectives, necessities and struggles of the working classes, which at the same time means fidelity to Marxism itself, above all by keeping in constant touch with the popular masses. (It must be borne in mind that one of the criticisms generally levelled against Latin American Marxists is that they do not maintain deep and continual contact with the masses.) Secondly, alliance with the Christians challenges Marxists to be coherent in the practice of solidarity with the exploited and oppressed. Finally, alliance with Christians should lead Marxists to abandon any remnant of sectarian positions. Very often the dogmatism of Marxist groups is shown less by their rejection of Christians than by incapacity to analyse the reality of each country in its own terms. Some impose on Latin American reality the analytical criteria which were correct in Russia in 1917 or in China in 1934, thus displaying the rigidity of a certain kind of thought, which is quite contrary to what Christians consider to be the commitment demanded of us by the Incarnation of Christ.

In short, Christians and Marxists, starting from their different standpoints, have gradually grown closer together until they have united in a revolutionary decision in favour of the liberation of the Latin American peoples. That process of growth is not at an end. We shall first consider what factors have made this mutual growth possible (what we might call points of agreement) and then examine the remaining problems which require the dialogue to be pursued in greater depth.

Basic points of agreement

In the first place there is not only agreement about the instruments of analysis to be applied to reality (the Marxist methods), but also about the data to which the analysis is applied. This has meant a change in the Marxist understanding of reality as well as in that of the Christians. As recently as ten years ago, in fact, Marxists regarded the problems of Latin America as a product of the basic contradiction between the 'modern' and the 'traditional'. They described Latin American society as affected by a 'structural dualism'. To overcome this, the process of 'modernization' was to be vigorously promoted, thus creating suitable conditions for the industrialization of the continent. This modernization was to be accompanied by a deliberate attempt at social participation which would make these societies more democratic. Education was regarded as a particularly valuable means of getting the whole process moving. The process would thus be evolutionary rather than one of conflict.

With the events which precipitated the establishment of socialism in Cuba and the subsequent analysis of those events, the Marxists revised their point of view. As a result the conviction grew, at first among Marxists regarded as 'heretics' but then also among 'official' Marxist thinkers, that Latin America's problems derive basically from the development of capitalism, which in its greed for gain has exploited and plundered Latin America. The root of the problem is to be found not in the opposition between the modern and the traditional, but between development and underdevelopment, between capital and forces of production, all of which finds expression in a series of conflicts, social tensions and class struggles which tend to get worse and worse.[9] The action of capitalism in creating underdevelopment in Latin America has created and reinforced structures of domination and dependence, not only in economic terms but also in social, cultural and above all political life. These structures exist not only in the relations between the Latin American countries and the capitalist countries on which they depend, but also in the internal social structures of the countries. Significant social change in Latin America is impossible unless this situation is overcome.

It is precisely this process of eliminating dependence that is denoted by the term 'liberation'. Latin American development must mean a break with the existing forms of domination and dependence. It will thus lead to forms of social and economic life which will have to be original. In other words, it is now accepted by Latin American Marxists that each country will have to find its own 'way' of development. Otherwise there will not be liberation but a continuation of the situation of dependence.

Dependence and liberation

Just as the Marxists' understanding has been changing, so Christians, too, now see the situation in Latin America as resulting from the domination of the great centres of world power. The *theology of liberation*

---

[9] Much has been written to illustrate this position. We recommend especially CARDOSO y FALETO, *Dependencia y Desarrollo en América Latina* ; Mexico : Siglo XXI, 1970. A. GUNDER FRANCK, *Capitalisme et sous-développement en Amérique latine*; Paris: Maspéro, 1968.

which is being worked out at present in Latin America makes awareness of dependence a central category in the study of the consciousness of liberation. Dependence and liberation are strictly related terms.

In short, Christians and Marxists approach reality with the same instruments of analysis, though from different standpoints and perspectives. Both agree in defining the Latin American situation as the product of domination that subjects these countries to dependence. To overcome this, liberation is imperative. The common revolutionary option translates into action the acceptance of this challenge.

Second, both partners in the dialogue agree in stressing the importance of the ethical factor. Cuban Marxists first, and then others in various Latin American countries, have indicated that while it is urgent to make structural changes in order to overcome conditions of dependence, so also it is fundamental to form a new man, capable of expressing in his personal life the new spirit which must accompany the development of the new society. It was Ernesto Guevara who most insisted on this point, stressing the need to forge this new personality by moral rather than material stimuli. Work ceases to be a burden for the human being and becomes an instrument of his liberation ; for that reason it is regarded as a 'social duty' which must be linked with 'technical development' (mastery of Nature) and which must be performed not just to earn wages but basically to build a new and just community. For that very reason it must be 'voluntary work'.[10] For Guevara, the two pillars which make possible the transition to communism are technical development and the new man, who is 'fuller, of great interior wealth and imbued with a sense of responsibility', who knows that 'he must sacrifice himself, because he lives in a time of sacrifice',[11] and above all, who is a revolutionary, '(. . .) guided by great feelings of love. It is impossible to think of an authentic revolutionary without this quality. This is perhaps one of the great dramas of a leader ; he must combine cool understanding with a passionate spirit, and take decisions, sometimes painful ones, without moving a muscle. Our avant-garde revolutionaries must idealize this love for the people, for the most sacred causes, to the point of making it a unique, indivisible thing.' [12]

Now the demand for human renewal, for conversion, is fundamental in the Christian message. The theologian José Míguez Bonino agrees.

---

[10] ERNESTO 'CHE' GUEVARA, *Le socialisme et l'homme à Cuba.* Havana : Institut du Livre, 1967, p. 30.
[11] *Ibid.,* p. 42.
[12] *Ibid.,* p. 43.

Only the free acceptance of the struggle can lead to responsible action. Yet authenticity as well as responsibility is expected of the Christian, and he must show this, not only by his dedication to just causes, but also through the consistency which will make him love and therefore give priority to the communal over the personal. For the Christian, life can only be lived in freedom (Gal. 5). But unlike Guevara and other Marxists, the Christian affirms that the new life of man is not the result of his own discipline, but a gift of God : the new man, in truth, is Jesus Christ :

'It would be difficult to exaggerate the importance of this biblical affirmation. What is at stake here is the very centre of the Gospel. God has not "required" humanity to attain authenticity, to renew itself : that would have been a new law and would have shut us even more into the circle of pride. God "gives us" true humanity, the new man. This is the axis on which the whole ethics of the Gospel turns : the new life, the good life, authentic life is not a demand, it is a gift. Jesus Christ is the new man.' [13]

But although there are differences about the origin of the newness of life, both Christians and Marxists agree that the 'new man' can only be such if he is free and lives in love.

Converging aims

In the third place, all this leads Christians and Marxists in Latin America today to join in a programme of ideological struggle, which they approach from different angles but with converging aims. Both understand that they must attack the problem set by the alienation from which the masses in Latin America suffer : poor, exploited, with no acceptable minimum standard of living, almost disqualified in their existence, yet unable to perceive the real causes of their ills. The dependence of Latin American countries on the centres of world capital and power is also reflected in the dependence of these long-exploited masses. This is why Marxists constantly strive by various means to create favourable conditions for a liberating awakening of consciousness. This involves establishing a programme of action on the ideological level.

Christians, too, know this situation of alienation at first hand. Not only do the vast Catholic masses suffer it, but also those grouped in the most

---

[13] José Míguez Bonino, *Ama y Haz lo que Quieras* ; Buenos Aires : La Aurora, 1972, p. 50. Cf. also by the same author the chapter 'Nuevas Perspectivas Teológicas' in the collective work *Pueblo Oprimido, Señor de la Historia* ; Montevideo : Tierra Nueva, 1972, p. 211.

popular evangelical denominations (for example the Pentecostals). According to Christian Lalive d'Epinay, who has made one of the best studies of Latin American Protestantism to date,

> 'These evangelical denominations reincarnated the past, prolonged it in the present. Hence our evangelical micro-societies may be regarded as :
>
> 1. Substitution societies at a time when the ancient social structures are disappearing but new ones have not appeared ;
> 2. Survivals (by their structure) adapted from the past ;
> 3. Societies that are closed, finished, without history, static.' [14]

Lalive d'Epinay, following this line of thought, speaks of a 'social strike of the Christians'. That is to say, their deliberate refusal to exercise the social responsibility which is theirs — a manifestation of the state of alienation from which they suffer. Hence the need to develop a programme designed to bring those who live in these conditions to a real awareness of their situation, their real needs and how to satisfy them.

The awakening of consciousness

The liberation of consciousness thus emerges as a common objective of Christians and Marxists on the ideological plane. It involves using various means to create conditions favourable to an awakening of class consciousness against which, it must be admitted, Christian faith has often been and continues to be manipulated.

The rigid stratification of Latin America societies makes unified popular mobilization difficult because it hides the common interests of the oppressed classes. There is a large sector of unemployed, with whom the industrial workers often do not recognize a basic community of interests. Racial differences, manipulated by those who are in power, also provoke a fragmentation of forces. Those who are opposed to change in Latin America know how to profit by all these elements in order to strengthen their domination. That is why Christians and Marxists who are committed to revolution have to work out a programme of action designed to get the people to share actively in the struggle for change. The Marxists, who have often mistakenly employed methods

---

[14] CHRISTIAN LALIVE D'EPINAY, 'La Iglesia Evangélica y la Revolución Latinoamericana', in : *Cristianismo y Sociedad*, No. 16/17, p. 26. Noel Olaya extends this analysis to the Catholic congregations in 'Unidad Cristiana y Lucha de Clases', in : *Pueblo Oprimido, Señor de la Historia*, p. 58.

of action which have separated them from the masses instead of getting the latter to take part in their own mobilization, have been occupied with this task for some time. But now the Christians are joining in as well. Hugo Assmann, for instance, can say :

> 'The fact that in Latin America liberation requires the removal of important obstacles present in the superstructure has a relevance for one fundamental element of the Christian faith. Man receives life as a gift, he is created from "outside" himself by God. This sounds vague, but it has very concrete implications which are closely related to our belief in revelation. Man does not spring spontaneously from the structures, although they provide the necessary material conditions for his "birth" as a new man. But if the material structures which provide the context shaping the consciousness of man do not add up to a process in which love is expressed through call and response, then what is generated is in fact a mere product of the structures and not the new man. In this sense the term Christian "witness" which has been emptied of its meaning retains its full force at the heart of the process of liberation. (. . .) This means that the Christian's influence will be related to the impact made by breaking the superstructure.' [15]

One of the methods which have been used to open breaches in the oppressed Christian consciousness is the liberating pedagogy of Paulo Freire. Its importance lies in the fact that goals and objectives have to be formulated on the basis of popular expectation, without any attempt to impose on the oppressed any preconceived idea of how to do things or of what to seek for by action. This method is also capable of correcting the mistaken views of people who want to work with the masses but in reality adopt a paternalist and therefore antiliberating attitude towards them. Freire's method emphasizes that in a true process of education and popular mobilization no one educates anyone else ; rather, all increase together in awareness of their class problems and of how they can be overcome. This has been and remains an especially appropriate method of carrying out the joint programme on the ideological level. It is clear that it is particularly important here, as we noted earlier, for Christians and Marxists to set aside *a priori* positions, sectarianism and dogmatic attitudes. Guevara pointed this out to the leading cadres in Cuba.[16]

---

[15] Hugo Assmann, 'The Christian Contribution to the Liberation of Spanish America', in : *Anticipation*, WCC, 1971, p. 25.

[16] Guevara, *op. cit.*, pp. 34-36.

To sum up this part of our essay, we can say that Christians and Marxists are agreed on a common goal : to overcome the flagrant injustices and social contradictions which characterize Latin American societies in order to establish a just society. For those who are committed to this process, the road that leads to this goal is that of socialism. As the Final Document of the Christians for Socialism meeting puts it :

> 'Socialism is the only acceptable means of overcoming class society. For classes are the reflection of the economic basis which in capitalist society creates an antagonistic division between the possessors of capital and the wage-earners. The latter have to work for the former and are thus an object of exploitation. Only by replacing private property by social ownership of the means of production can objective conditions be created for the suppression of class antagonism.' [17]

Open questions

Agreement on such matters as action, tactical and strategic alliances and joint programmes of ideological struggle is not sufficient to overcome all the problems which can arise in a dialogue between Christians and Marxists. But as we have already noted, such problems need not separate them, but can prompt both partners to deeper reflection. Christians and Marxists call each other to be more faithful to their essential bases, and this has led to a restatement of both Christian faith and Marxism. In this process Christians discover anew that faith is not restricted to the inner life of a human being, disembodied and separated from action and social responsibility. Consequently, Christians try to understand the Gospel on the basis of the context of conflict in which they live, and this obliges them not only to make a choice but also to engage in specific political activity.

> 'Another element of this restatement of faith (...) is the political dimension of faith. Faith cannot be political, since it is a matter of giving concrete form to our love of man by taking a stand in favour of the struggle of the people. When we speak of "political action" in this context, it is no longer a question of the seizure and exercise of power by a group, but of the total struggle, with the aim of creating a socialist society in which the people call the moves. It is also a question of a transformation of man as a whole, in all his dimensions. Faith has a part to play in this process, opening him to the gift of God.' [18]

---

[17] *Cristianos por el Socialismo*, p. 295.
[18] *Ibid.*, pp. 269-270.

Christian identity

This reformulation of faith leads to a thorough examination of ecclesiological questions within the context of a common struggle for liberation. There are, of course, many Christians who once opted for revolutionary commitment but gradually abandoned the Church — they 'lost their faith'. But there are also many, very many more in fact, who still declare themselves Christians and who maintain their militant devotion to liberation. Both, however, are agreed on one point: the Church's traditional forms of life no longer seem valid to those who are trying to express the faith in the present revolutionary Latin American context. Míguez Bonino, who deals with this problem particularly well, notes:

> 'Perhaps the gravest disagreements among Christians dedicated to the process of liberation arise in regard to their attitudes to the institutions and objective celebrations of Christian faith, which range from uncritical and sometimes fervent participation at one extreme to systematic refusal to take part in any liturgical form of worship or institutional aspects of the life of the Church including critical participation or the creation of substitute groups and forms of celebration. (...) In fact, the Christian who reflects on his practice in terms of socio-political analysis and of the facts which give him his identity as a Christian is located (however "incarnate" his reflection may be) within two circles of consciousness, not concentric but intersecting. Both are essentially communal. And, in my view, the one cannot be substituted for the other. But participation in both in the present situation (and we cannot speak of any other) inevitably involves conflict to a greater or lesser extent. It is this, it seems to me, and not some subtle theoretical question, which is the real ecclesiological problem. And here again, it will not be resolved by speculation but by concrete commitment. In other words, the Latin American revolutionary Christian has to solve the problem of his church practice, without which his Christian identity is incomplete.' [19]

While Christians are restating their faith, the Marxists are undergoing a similar process of reflection. If anything is clear in the dialogue, it is that the Marxists are not maintaining their theoretical and political position with the dogmatism of earlier times, but are showing themselves increasingly ready to consider the problems of Latin America without seeking to judge them from perspectives which perhaps were correct in other contexts but have no universal validity. In reality the dialogue has served to bring the Marxists themselves to greater openness, since they

---

[19] José Míguez Bonino, 'Nuevas Perspectivas Teológicas', *loc. cit.*, pp. 211-212.

have found that faith is not an obstacle to revolutionary struggle. Some Marxists are beginning to reconsider Marx's criticism of religion. This is a subject which needs deeper study, since it is common to Christians and Marxists. Nevertheless, the events which have produced the nucleus of revolutionary Christians demonstrate that the Christian element can serve the cause of liberation.[20]

The class struggle

A second problem has been raised but has not yet been solved: the relation of the Church to the class struggle, or, rather, the Church in the context of class struggle. One clear feature of Marxist conduct in the last ten years in regard to the Latin American Church has been a firm will not to attack the Church, nor to set it in opposition to the revolution,[21] since Christians are seen as strategical allies. This implies that the Marxists believe the Christian community has a role to play in the class struggle: in reality this matter is more serious for Christians than for Marxists. For Marxists, the class struggle is the very texture of history, whereas for Christians the Church is the place where human divisions are overcome, since in Christ 'there is neither slave nor free; Jew nor Greek'. How then can a Christian take part in the revolution, the clearest expression of the class war? How can he act against others who also call themselves Christians? Given that Christ unites human beings, how is it that Christians, as Christians, can take part in division and conflict? Is this not to admit that Jesus Christ unites some but divides others? But according to the testimony of the Gospel and the New Testament, the unity of Christ is the unity of all. Discussing this problem, Fr Noel Olaya of Colombia notes:

> 'The unity of Christ, in its fullness, is the unity of all; this unity in process of realization, on the other hand, demands choices, and by that very fact it cannot fail to create division. And these choices at the level of what we call "worldly" matters, are political, economic, and so one. The important thing, therefore, is the criterion which guides them.
> The basic criterion in this case is a commitment to the poor and oppressed, by adopting their aspirations of freedom and by dedication to their struggle. "The problem of the unity of the Church cannot be separated

---

[20] Cf. HUGO ASSMANN, *op. cit.* Another reappraisal prompted by the Christian-Marxist dialogue concerns the method of doing theology in this new situation. In this regard the work of JOSÉ MÍGUEZ BONINO, 'Nuevas Perspectivas Teológicas', *loc. cit.*, is extremely valuable.

[21] Cf. F. CASTRO, *op. cit.*, p. 268.

from the problem of the unity of the world", says Fr Giulio Girardi. The two roads to unity go by way of the liberation of the poor.' [22]

The understanding of the unity of the Church as referring to the unity and justice which God has given to men in Christ has brought revolutionary Christians in Latin America to see the class struggle as the 'struggle against organized hatred'.[23] For them, then, the class struggle is an instrument through which Christian love can be shown no longer as a simple relation between an I and a Thou, but between those who constitute the people, the community, *us*. When the Church is aware of what the class struggle involves, it will undergo a process of reconversion which will eventually make it possible to overcome the division between clergy and laity, and to democratize church life, thus enabling Christianity to regain the revolutionary drive of the early Church. This obviously presupposes a questioning of the Church as an agent of social conciliation, and at the same time it prompts the Church to examine its own conscience, in case it resembles the 'prophets' of the Old Testament who spoke of peace when there was no peace.

A third unsolved problem for many revolutionary Christians is posed by the use of violence. There are some who have already decided the matter by opting for violence or non-violence. Clearly this problem does not arise for the Marxist conscience ; their position is well known ('Violence is the mother of history' — Marx). But for Christians who are committed to liberation, the problem of violence is inescapable. For some, it arises at the level of principles and ethical choices ; for others, it must be examined in the light of tactical demands. Every effort must be made to avoid the risk of identifying violence (a means) with liberation (the end). At the same time, however, it is imperative to lay aside 'the shallow sentimentality which passes for Christian ethics in these matters, hiding reactionary attitudes under basic theological categories like reconciliation, forgiveness or peace, which in the long run are more costly in human lives and suffering and less respectful of the human person'.[24] When humane criteria are applied, violence can be an instrument of liberation from structural violence. But this means submitting the use of violence to the requirements of political and social struggles.

---

[22] NOEL OLAYA, *loc. cit.*, pp. 66-67.

[23] *Cristianos por el Socialismo*, p. 268.

[24] JOSÉ MÍGUEZ BONINO, 'La Violencia : Una Reflexión Teológica', in : *Cristianismo y Sociedad*, Montevideo, 1971, No. 28, p. 10. English : 'Violence — a theological reflection', in *The Ecumenical Review*, Vol. XXV, No. 4, October 1973, p. 468.

Conclusion

Events in Chile since 11 September 1973 put to the test the effectiveness of the alliance between Christians and Marxists and of their common struggle. In fact, they call in question the whole activity of the Latin American Left. It is not possible here to deal fully with this subject, but it points to a problem of which Christians and Marxists are not always aware, namely that if their struggle is to be really effective it will take a long time, and it will demand great patience. Above all, they must realize that there is no place for hopes of miraculous change. The struggle for a new society will inevitably demand huge sacrifice, a love which will not admit weakness and the cultivation of a hope which must not be confused with illusion. On this, Christians and Marxists are in full agreement.

SOME REFLECTIONS ON AFRICAN EXPERIENCE OF SALVATION TODAY

JOHN MBITI[1]

1. Introduction

The word 'salvation' has a long history, because man has always searched for salvation in one form or another. All religions of the world have also addressed themselves to the question of human salvation, and have provided different answers to it. Salvation is never outdated : it is always 'salvation today', for each generation of people.

This paper is treated in two sections. The first part is an analysis of the linguistic and religious meaning of salvation in the traditional African setting. The second part discusses African responses to the Christian message of salvation. The reason for looking at these responses is that two-thirds of Africa are rapidly embracing the Christian Faith and we are witnessing the transformation of the notion of salvation from the traditional African background to a new and Christian understanding. This is one of the most fruitful areas of religious interaction in contemporary Africa.

2. African background to the theme of salvation

a) *Linguistic considerations*

Since the Christian proclamation of salvation is carried out in different languages of the world, some analysis of the linguistic settings of salvation and related terms is necessary at one point or another. It is very possible that the missionary or local convert or evangelist, would be proclaiming salvation in a given language without fully appreciating the cultural and social background of the words he uses in his proclamation. Thus he might imagine that he is saying one thing, while the listeners understand a different thing from the same proclamation. As of the end of 1972, the Bible had been translated, in full or in part, into nearly 600 African languages ; and no doubt the preaching of the Gospel was or is being carried out in many more languages in Africa. I shall take only one of these languages, Kikamba, which I know best, and consider some of the words used in preaching the Gospel and in the translation of the Bible. It is spoken by about 1,500,000 Akamba people in Kenya.

i) The abstract nouns *utangiio* (salvation) and *wovosyo* (redemption) are practically never used outside of the Christian context. I have not

---

[1] Canon Professor Mbiti was previously Head of the Department of Religious Studies, Makerere University, Uganda. He is now Director of the Ecumenical Institute, Bossey.

come across ther abstract usage in traditional life other than within the Christian proclamation. This would mean, among other things, that the hearer must be able to apply the word salvation or redemption in practical terms, if it is to have any personal meaning to him.

ii) Similarly the words *mwovosya* (redeemer) and *mutangiii* (saviour), as concrete nouns, are rarely used in Akamba background, and even then in completely non-technical ways. If someone 'saves' another person from danger, he is in effect his 'saviour', but people would not call him saviour or redeemer since he acted that way because of the particular moment of emergency. Once the act is over, he does not continue in the capacity of 'saving'; therefore he cannot earn the title or name saviour (mutangiii). There is no profession of saving or redeeming people. There are no (and never have been) traditional saviours or redeemers.

iii) Thirdly we consider the verbs *kutangiia* (to save) and *kwovosya* (to redeem). This is where action takes place. *Kutangiia* (to save) functions in many areas : God saves the sick from death, people from danger, calamity, destruction, famine, drought, war, animals, drowning, floods, locusts, and captivity. Saving is always a present reality, and God steps in where and when human powers fail or prove inadequate. People exclaim in joy, after escaping from danger, 'Oh, were it not for God, I would now be dead !' Or, when suddenly confronted with danger, one would call loudly upon God, 'Our God !' or 'My God !', thereby appealing to Him to intervene and save the person from danger. When a sick person grows worse and worse and nears the end of life, in spite of all attempts to cure him, people say, *Mundu ni wa Ngai* (the person is now God's — meaning, that it is now up to God to save him from death) ; or they would say that the person 'is now in the hands of God' (meaning that only God's intervention will rescue him from death). When such a person recovers, people may say, 'Ah, God took him out of a terrible place', or 'only God could have saved him.'

A man saves another person or an animal from danger, water, flood, wild animals, accident, and so on. He may also rescue an article of property from fire, loss or destruction.

A dog may also save someone or something from danger, from attack or other situation which would have led to loss or death. A branch of a tree saves someone from falling to his death ; the discovery of a well of water saves a traveller from dying of thirst ; a log of wood floating in the water saves a swimmer from drowning ; new information saves a person from an otherwise unnecessary journey or effort.

The words redeemer, redeem and redemption, for which the Kikamba equivalents are *mwovosya*, *kwovosaya*, *wovosyo*, respectively, are not commonly used in Akamba life. The word 'to redeem' is used when something has been captured by someone else and the owner wants it back. Then he pays a goat, cow, or another article, to the one who had captured his property, and he gets it back that way. This is more an arrangement of convenience than anything to do with religion. Situations that call for it are extremely rare. It is an exclusively human activity which never applies to God, animals or anything else 'redeeming' something or someone.

The preaching of the Gospel through the missionary enterprise in Africa, has precipitated the use of these terms in a technical sense. Indeed it may be said that Christian evangelization has been executed around the concepts of Saviour, Salvation, Redeemer and Redemption. Local African words have been borrowed and used in different parts of the continent to translate these terms and to apply them in evangelism and Church life. What the words mean in the traditional linguistic and cultural setting, has clearly a bearing on the way in which the Christian concept of salvation is understood and applied by the people concerned.

b) *Salvation in African religion*

Linguistic considerations do not yield a great deal of the meaning of the term salvation, at least in the Kikamba language. We ask, however, whether African traditional religious life, has the concept of salvation. We might say from the start that many of the practical expressions of African religion, all over the continent, are basically salvatory. These are particularly prayers, offerings and sacrifices made towards God and sometimes towards other spiritual realities. They arise out of the feeling of man's need for help which comes from outside of his own abilities. African religion is rich in these acts. The majority of prayers in African Religion are petitions, requests, and intercessions, for health, healing from disease and barrenness, for success (hence salvation from failure) in undertakings, protection from harm and danger or death ; others are for peace and blessings — hence salvation from war, from deprivation. The times that necessitate prayer are fundamentally times that call for salvation — drought, sickness, danger, undertakings, start of the day or of the night, marriage, birth, and even death. Prayers of thanksgiving are an expression of gratitude for saving acts — for example at harvest time, after a drought, after childbirth, after recovery from danger or sickness, for God's kindness and mercy shown in particular ways. Blessings that are so often invoked upon people in African societies, generally appealing to God to do the actual blessing, also indicate people's desire for the best, the good, that which saves and keeps safe or prosperous.

As an illustration of these prayers we take one from the Galla of Ethiopia and Kenya. This prayer is recited in the morning, soliciting God's salvatory help in the course of the day.

'O God, it is in peace that I have rested,
Make me pass the day in peace
You have prepared in peace the way I have followed,
Make me pass the day in peace.
Make me walk straight on this road (that is, safely)
If I speak, take calumny from my lips
If I hunger, take away my pride
May I pass this day in calling upon you,
O Master that knows no other master.'

Sacrifices and offerings are made in all African societies, within Traditional Religion. Whatever theories of interpreting them may be put forward, the basic idea behind them is to acknowledge the saving acts of God and spiritual beings as the case might be. Man wants to be safe in an otherwise insecure world of sickness, death, droughts, floods, accidents, epidemics, misfortunes, witchcraft, malevolent spirits, etc. In former years the sacrificing of human beings was carried out in a number of African societies : some of the victims offered themselves to be sacrificed ; others were forced to be sacrificed, from among their communities ; while other individuals were captured from neighbouring tribes and then sacrificed. Only major communal or national needs necessitated the sacrificing of human beings ; and the aim of doing so was to have one or more persons die in order that the majority would be saved from calamity, drought, war or other adversity.

Furthermore, there are and have been in many African societies, shrines, sacred mountains or rocks or caves which people consider as providing safety for human beings and animals and birds. Any person, or animal hiding himself or found in such sacred places, may not be killed — the sacred places in effect save life from destruction even if paradoxically they are also the places where sacrifices are made. The point is that the concept of salvation is thereby given a geographical concretization : it is not just an abstraction.

God is regarded as being ultimately the saviour of people and the other living things since he is their Creator. He may not always have that as one of his titles, but other names and sayings about him indicate clearly that people regard Him to be the ultimate saviour. He is the Giver of Life (thus saving man from death); the Giver of Rain or Water (thus saving man and nature from drought and shortage of water); He is the Protector of the Poor (Rutangaboro, among Barundi, who also call him *Ntirandekuva* which means, 'He has not let me drop yet'); to the Ila of Zambia, God is *Luvhunabaumba* (which means, 'Deliverer of those in trouble'); and for some He is known as Saviour or Deliverer. But, the fact that prayers of petitions for help are so commonly addressed to God, shows that people regard Him to be their saviour — at least in practical terms, even if that term may rarely be used of him in a technical or formal way.

In addition to the content of salvation in prayers and sacrifices, there are other sayings about God by which people indicate their feelings towards him as the one who keeps them safe. A proverb in Rwanda and Burundi says: 'A tree (or young plant) protected by God cannot be hurt by the wind'. This saying means that one is absolutely safe in the hands of God. The Ila of Zambia say: 'God has long arms', by which it is meant that the arms of God symbolize the care, protection and security provided by him. One of the names of God used by the Akan of Ghana is *Abommubuwafre* which means 'He upon whom you call in your experience of distress: a Consoler or Comforter who gives salvation'.

In African oral history and myths, it is told how God intervened and saved people from great calamity, famine, war, flood or other destructive forces of nature. The Meru of Kenya narrate that at one time the people were enslaved in bondage, and then God raised a leader (Mugwe) who, with the help of God, saved and brought them out of bondage to their present land. This story is cast rather like the Exodus story of the children of Israel, but it is not known whether or not the two have a remote connection.

In these religious considerations of the concept of *Salvation*, we take note that salvation in African Religion has to do with physical and immediate dangers (of the individual and more often of the community) — dangers that threaten individual or community survival, good health, and general prosperity or safety. This is the main religious setting in which the notion of salvation is understood and experienced. Salvation is not just an abstraction: it is concrete, told in terms of both what has happened and is likely to be encountered by people as they go through daily experiences. Therefore, as understood through African religious experiences in the traditional setting, salvation is either past or present. This is basically in keeping with the general African understanding of time which lays great emphasis on the past and the present.

Another important point about salvation in the African background is that it rarely, if ever, has to do with what we may call sin or the moral life of the individual or his community. Even though in effect salvation in physical situations brings peace of mind, a sense of security, increase of life, these are the psychological results of salvation ; people do not ask to be saved from an 'evil' of a moral nature, or one which may have intervened between God and man. There are myths and stories all over Africa which tell how, in the primeval period, God and men lived in close proximity, which was paradise for man since God supplied him with all that he needed (food, safety and shelter). The myths go on to tell how this closeness was broken up when, in various ways, man did something wrong the consequence of which was that God withdrew himself geographically to the sky or heavens. Some myths even say that death came to the world ; others that man lost the gifts of immortality, resurrection and rejuvenation. There are no myths that tell how the lost physical proximity between God and man, or the lost gifts, would ever be recovered. Man just accepted the situation as it turned out to be, and has lived with it since then. Through prayers, sacrifices and offerings, man still approaches God, and God provides for man's needs in various ways. Through marriage and procreation, man fights against death, thereby keeping death under some measure of control.

While these stories of the separation between God and man, and the coming of death to the world, have some resemblance with the Genesis story of the so-called Fall of Man, we must emphasize that in African Religion they do not speak of moral estrangement between God and man — in the way that the Genesis story has so often been interpreted to mean. The question of original sin is, therefore, out of place as far as African Religion is concerned. Similarly the question of salvation from moral evil is also out of question. African Religion in this respect, did not produce the concept of spiritual redemption or salvation. There was no logical necessity, in the context of African Religion, for God to intervene in a personal and cosmic way, in human history, to bring a new course of human history whose goal in the future will be a consummation of history, a salvation of mankind, a new creation of all things in Christ and the establishment of the Kingdom of God. That cosmic outreach of salvation is unknown and would be impossible within the context of African religious heritage.

We have taken a lot of space and time to speak of salvation in the African religious and traditional background. This is necessary because it is extremely relevant to what we are going to say as we analyse African understanding and experience of salvation within the Christian context today.

3. African understanding and experience of Christian salvation

We have seen that both linguistically and religiously, the idea of salvation is very much present in African life, even if the abstract concepts related to it may be rare or non-existent as such. This means that Christianity did not introduce the concept of salvation as something uniquely new except in so far as salvation is mediated in and through Christ. The need for salvatory acts has always been there in African societies. When Christianity spoke of salvation, therefore, it struck a familiar note in a very needy area in the life and experiences of African peoples all over the continent. This means that, whether or not African understanding of salvation in Christianity is theologically sound, the very fact of speaking about salvation, saviour, saving, redeemer, redemption, and redeeming, makes the Christian Faith deeply meaningful and relevant to African hearers of the Gospel. If Christianity lacked salvation (however the word might be understood) and its related concepts or implications, it would have lacked a serious element in the religious and experiential yearnings of African peoples. The fact that it had *that* as one of its most important, indeed as its most central element, has meant that something 'clicked' with African peoples. They had already been prepared for it, and their daily experiences forced them to take note, whatever interpretations may be accorded to that word by the different evangelizing agents and Churches and schools of theology, and however they were to receive, interpret and apply that concept. We take serious note in passing, that Christianity is spreading now more rapidly in two-thirds of Africa than it has ever done on such a large scale in all its two thousand-years history. This is happening within a relatively short period since Christianity began to penetrate Africa during the last 70 to 150 years, and precisely where African Religion has been most predominant. It can be argued that this African Religion prepared the ground for the rapid and often ready accommodation of the Christian Message — a message which is basically one of salvation. Christianity has come to African peoples to bring more abundantly what in daily life they felt and needed most. It has come to *legitimize their case* and to bring an extended understanding, scope and applicability of salvation.

African Christians within the historical churches have followed more or less the teachings of those churches concerning salvation, all of which emphasize the notion of sin and man's need to be rescued from that. Whether this is the only legitimate usage or interpretation of salvation in the Bible, is not for us to consider here ; I am only stating it as a historical fact that evangelization in Africa has stressed the idea of salvation only from sin. But there are also independent churches in Africa which have broken off from mission or historical churches, and others from one another. It is in these free Churches that we find a wider range of African people's understanding and experience of salvation in the Christian context.

The fact that Jesus is the Son of God, that He took on human form and lived among men and worked miracles of healing, rescuing, raising the dead, and so on, is extremely meaningful to African Christians. The combination of God and Man is a revolutionary factor in African religious experience. Jesus personalizes the almightiness of God to save, and brings that personal almightiness of God on to the level of daily experiences. Whereas in African traditional life, people look or appeal to God as the final resort when help is most desperately needed, in Christian experience the personalization of the almightiness of God makes it possible for the Christian to appeal to God, in Jesus, as both the first and final resort. Therefore, in the Christian experience, one may enter through faith into a relationship with God or Jesus, or both, which guarantees an abiding and undiminishing state of rescue and protection. The Christian becomes a member of those who have been 'rescued', those who constitute a 'safe' flock which nothing can threaten since it is under the protection of the personalized almightiness of God. In the Christian schema, Jesus is often referred to as Saviour although, incidentally, the New Testament very rarely uses this as one of the titles of Jesus. Therefore, this Jesus who is so human, and at the same time Saviour, is able to enter into all human situations which call for salvation. Thus, African peoples find salvation to be meaningful in areas far beyond the limitations of evangelical theology which has more or less confined that term to the question of sin.

What then are some of the situations in which salvation is meaningful to African Christians ? Sickness is one of the commonest experiences in African societies. Therefore salvation for many African Christians must mean healing, and it is no wonder that a lot of the Independent Churches put great emphasis on healing. For example, the African Apostolic Church of Johane Maranke (Zimbabwe), has a hierarchy of officers parallel to that of the episcopalians, but this hierarchy starts at the top with the Healer, then Prophet, Baptizer and Evangelist (as the lowest in the scale). Healing sessions in Independent Churches form one of the most important services of worship, some of them going on for up to four hours at a time. There are churches which forbid their members to use any form of medicine, whether from the hospitals or traditional medicine men, telling them to rely only on the healing work of God through Christ Jesus.

There are many areas of need for salvation and we can only enumerate them without going into details. They include witchcraft, misfortune, danger, magic, sorcery, barrenness, troublesome spirits, calamity, unemployment, the state of unmarried life, and death, as far as individual life is concerned. For community, they include : drought, war, oppression, foreign domination, slavery, locust invasion, epidemics, floods, storms, earthquakes, and so on. This is the wide range to which the notion of salvation has been and must be stretched, to be fully meaningful as Africans experience the Christian faith in the day to day life. These areas of need come out clearly in conversation, in the hymns sung and prayers offered by African Christians especially in the Independent Churches. This list of situations needing salvation is very similar to the one in the traditional setting of life. The question of salvation from sin arises mainly in so far as sin is somehow in the category of these other dilemmas of life. And here we take note of the fact that in traditional African life, sin (i.e. what constitutes sin) is fundamentally horizontal in the sense that it is injury to the relationships between individuals, and rarely is it ever seen in terms of vertical offence against God. Therefore, as far as sin is concerned, salvation has to do with the removal of injured relationships on a horizontal and human plane.

If African Christians were not able to apply the concept of salvation to concrete and physical dilemmas of their existence, they would, by far and large, have rejected the Christian message. As it is now, they have been able to stretch that concept to suit their needs and according to their understanding. This does not mean that they are not saved from sin, nor that we should gloss over the question of sin in its spiritual dimension. But for African Christians, Christ comes as Saviour, transporting the almightiness of God the Father, to save from everything, including sin.

We could sum up these considerations by saying that African experience of the Christian concept of salvation has underscored the areas of salvatory needs as found in traditional African life and religion ; and only within those needs has the idea of salvation from sin also found a place. Sin becomes one of the many ills and dilemmas needing the intervention of God as much as the physical dilemmas. But, at the same time, the Christian concept of salvation is projected in a future-ward direction to cover the safety and security of the believer in the next life which, for Christians, is expected to be lived in heaven, the home of God. The idea of salvation extending to the hereafter is probably the main new element in African experience of Christian salvation since it promises to do something which African Religion never contained or never could do even if it were to see the need, namely the recovery of the intimate proximity between God and man which was in the original state of human existence. At the same time, Christian salvation promises the recovery of the lost gifts of rejuvenation, immortality and resurrection — thus banishing death once and forever. These dimensions of Christian salvation, though somewhat vague by being cast in a mythological and futurist language, have a cherished place in the hearts of many African Christians : they constitute a new hope, the Christian hope without which, perhaps, the experience of salvation for the present alone would have only a limited attraction and meaningfulness. But as it is, Christian salvation sweeps over the physical and spiritual welfare of the believers, and applies as well for this life as for the life to come. This message has found a home in African Christians, and some have died for it, many more will be willing to die for it, and thousands of them are proclaiming it every day, every month and every year.

4. Areas that need further application of salvation today

Space prevents us from considering in any detail or depth, the many areas and situations that demand salvatory attention in African Christianity today. So far we have spoken of the way people apply their understanding of salvation. In this section we should address ourselves to those areas where salvation is also needed, whether people are aware of it or not. But they are necessary of inclusion as the Church grows and matures in Africa. We can do no more than enumerate them very briefly and quickly.

i) Salvation and African cultural heritage. Our cultural heritage like the cultures of other peoples of the world, has its weaknesses and strong points. We need to be saved from the cultural demons, fallacies, fears, hatreds, prejudices and structures of our heritage. At the same time, Christian salvation must mean rescuing the good, the valuable, the holy, the pure, the noble, the best, out of our cultural heritage in order to preserve it and disseminate it. Thus, salvation within the African cultural heritage must mean redeeming and sanctifying the good and destroying the evil.

ii) The Church in Africa is in desperate need of salvation, even if it claims to be made up of those who have come to accept Christian salvation. What is needed here is salvation from worn out structures inherited from Europe and America, from outdated traditions, from domination by overseas brethren who have the money and the power, from arrogance, paternalism and even racism which have often gone hand in hand with missionaries. It needs salvation from the position of inferiority in the sight of the so-called older churches ; and from the loss of dignity as long as we are considered poor, underdeveloped, needy (of material goods) and always at the receiving end.

iii) Salvation from the present state of church life should point towards integration, maturity, selfhood, dignity and service, as a viable Church in Africa which comes under the direct leading of the Holy Spirit and not of imaginary human leadership.

iv) Christian salvation in Africa must also address itself to areas of human life which are desperate. These are innumerable and we can only cite a few. The racism of southern Africa, colonial subjugation of African peoples by European foreigners in Rhodesia and South Africa, and Arabs in the north, are clear examples where on a large scale, Christian salvation must say something, must do something. It is for this reason that there are those Christians in Africa and elsewhere who can only understand salvation in the context of political liberation — and who can blame them ? Yet, the Church in Africa as a whole, has not begun to take seriously the liberation dimension of salvation. There are also local situations of national life that need salvation, especially what now goes by the terms 'tribalism', 'corruption', 'nepotism' and the like. Modern forms of life have their own demons from which African peoples need to be saved, such as empty ideologies, materialism, atheism, economic exploitation, and so on.

v) There is, finally, the cosmic dimension of salvation which must be given its place in African Christianity. So far, in the day-to-day experiences of salvation, emphasis has been laid on mainly the individual and the community. This dimension is necessary and meaningful when considering the personalization of salvation. True theological perspectives of salvation in the New Testament embrace the cosmic consequences of the Christ event. This cosmicization of salvation does not seem to attract the attention of the majority of African Christians. But to understand or take Christian salvation only on a community or personal level, is ultimately to ignore its cosmic dimension and thereby to distort the Christian message seriously. In its major concern with saving souls, evangelization in Africa has noticeably ignored the cosmic dimension of salvation. Only the Orthodox Church in Ethiopia and Egypt, like other Orthodox Churches, has maintained in its liturgies, the recognition of the cosmic dimension of salvation. It seems necessary to explore the implications of the cosmic work of Christ within the African context and in the light of African cosmology. In that cosmic sweep it may well become clear that in a limited way, the African traditional experiences of salvation belong ultimately within the walls of the cosmic work of Christ.